6 WAYS TO LIVE A MORE SELF- RELIANT LIFE

6 WAYS TO LIVE A MORE SELF-RELIANT LIFE

RENEE MCCORRY

Cover by German Creative

Disclaimers:

This document is intended for entertainment and educational purposes only. The author makes no warranties, guarantees, or implications of any kind. The reader acknowledges that the author is not providing legal, medical, financial, or professional advice. It is recommended to consult a qualified professional before attempting any techniques or projects mentioned in this book. The reader also acknowledges that the author is not liable for any losses incurred directly or indirectly from the use of the information in this document, including any errors, omissions, or inaccuracies. First Printing, 2025

Contents

To my dear friend Cheral,

You gave me back my love for reading, leading to me once again

put pen to paper (or fingers to keyboard). You inspire me with

your courage to fight for my dreams and to live the life God gave

me to the fullest. Your strength and faith are inspiring to

everyone you meet. You will always be in my heart.

Preface

So, you're thinking about embracing a more self-reliant life? That's awesome! Welcome aboard, friend. I've spent years, okay, a couple of decades, experiencing the rewards and disappointments of the homesteading life. I went from a one-bedroom apartment with a patio to a suburban backyard. And let me tell you, it's been an adventure.

Let's clarify something. Being self-reliant is not about becoming a hermit in the woods, although when 5:00 o'clock traffic hits, I admit it has its appeal. It's about gaining skills and knowledge that empower you, make you more resilient, and allow you to live more self-sufficiently.

Let me start off by stating that this book is not just a collection of recipes and gardening tips; it's a toolbox filled with practical advice, inspiring stories (some slightly embarrassing), and a hefty dose of encouragement. I am all about encouraging others to embrace a lifestyle that relies less on commercial farming and more on local and backyard growing.

Whether you're a seasoned gardener or have never so much as planted a sunflower seed, you'll find something here to convince you to get your hands dirty, in the best possible way. I believe that less stuffy textbooks and more campfire chats with knowledgeable and slightly quirky friends are the way to learn.

Prepare to open your mind to an old-fashioned, turned trendy way of living, starting where you are.

Introduction

Self-reliance and self-sufficiency both relate to a person's ability to function independently. However their focus differs.

Self-reliance is about the internal capacity and confidence to man- age one's life.
Self-sufficiency is more about the external ability to provide for oneself.

You may think they have nothing in common. Two completely different sides of the mirror. But they go hand-in-hand. You see they are like a dynamic duo. They each have their own superpowers. I realized that while they have their unique focuses, they often work together.

I can be self-reliant and trust my instincts to make decisions, but that didn't mean I couldn't also be self-sufficient and learn about how to go about what my instincts are telling me and provide for my needs. By practicing both, you get the best of both worlds.

You will have the confidence to take on challenges and the practicality to back it up.

In a world that often feels disconnected and dependent on self-serving and potentially harmful systems, the pursuit of self-reliance offers the choice of a more fulfilling and sustainable existence.

Think of this book as your guide on that journey. My goal is to lead you towards a deeper understanding of self-sufficiency and empower you with some practical skills to achieve it.

We'll explore the nature of self-reliance and move past the misunderstood notion that complete isolation is required to embrace a healthier and peaceful life.

For me, it's about cultivating resilience and resourcefulness, the ability to grow your own food, nurture your own well-being naturally, and reduce your environmental impact—while leading your family towards the comfort of a more natural lifestyle.

This book dives into the practical aspects of self-sufficiency, from establishing a thriving garden in even the smallest of spaces to mastering the art of preserving your harvest and creating your own chemical-free health and beauty products.

I want to help you tackle your own challenges and offer solutions for those with limited resources, time, or space. I would like to show you that self-reliance is attainable for anyone, regardless of their circumstances.

With clear instructions, helpful recipes, and a healthy dose of hu- mor, this guide will transform you from a novice to a confident homesteader one step at a time.

I can confidently say I do not know everything there is to know about homesteading. In fact, like you, I am learning and growing in my knowledge of this rewarding journey of self-reliance. So, roll up your sleeves, gather your tools, and let's get started!

One

Embracing the Self-Reliant Lifestyle

Defining Self-Reliance

Mikhail Nilov

Okay, let's start by ditching the misconception that self-reliance means becoming a hermit in the woods, surviving solely on dandelion greens and rainwater gathered in a banana leaf. Though, admittedly, dandelion greens *are* surprisingly versatile!

In today's interconnected world, self reliance takes on a more skewed meaning. It's really not about complete isolation from society, but rather about embracing a sense of empowerment and resilience.

It's about equipping yourself with the knowledge and skills to navigate life's bumps in the road with confidence and independence. Not to mention reducing your dependence on external systems, and strengthening your ability to thrive. But most of all it's about building community.

Think of it like this; a sturdy oak tree stands tall, all while weathering storms and droughts. It doesn't isolate itself from the forest, but it doesn't rely solely on the forest either. It has deep roots, strong branches, and the ability to adapt to changing conditions. That, my friends, is the essence of modern self-reliance. It's about building your own strong roots, developing adaptable branches, and knowing how to weather the storms that comes your way.

This mindset extends far beyond simply surviving. It touches on every aspect of your well-being. Reducing reliance on government systems and commercial farming will lead to greater security.

Imagine the savings from reducing your grocery bill by growing a large portion of your own food.

I have an entire freezer dedicated to vegetables I grew and froze for the winter, as well as shelves of foods I canned from my gar- den. This gives me peace of mind knowing despite any kind of weather related, governmental, or financial unrest my family will be taken care of (and a few friends who laid claim to my home in uncertain times).

What about other skills other than gardening? Imagine being more handy where you can mend a broken chair instead of immediately replacing it. This financial independence translates into reduced stress and increased freedom.

Furthermore, a self-reliant lifestyle often leads to a healthier and more fulfilling life. The act of growing your own food, preparing meals from scratch, and engaging in physical activity like gardening, connects you to nature and fosters a deeper appreciation for the food you consume.

This connection often leads to healthier eating habits and a greater awareness of where your food comes from and how it is grown.

Conscious consumerism significantly benefits both your personal well-being and the planet's delicate ecosystem.

Consider the environmental impact. By reducing your reliance on mass produced goods, environment damaging packaging, and transportation, you're significantly decreasing your carbon foot- print and contributing to a more sustainable planet.

Then there is the satisfaction of making your own products. From cleaning solutions to body lotions, it really is a deeply gratifying and creative process. Imagine knowing exactly what goes into the products you use. To be sure they exclude harmful chemicals and ensure ethical sourcing. This can provide an incredible sense of control and well-being. It's a quiet revolution, one jar, one garden bed, one repaired item at a time.

But let's not paint a picture of unrealistic perfection. Self-reliance isn't about achieving complete autonomy overnight. It's an ongoing journey specifically designed for your lifestyle and the needs of your family. It will take time. It's about taking baby steps, celebrating small victories along the way and acknowledging that setbacks are simply opportunities for learning and growth. It's about embracing the imperfections and finding joy in the process.

Many might think that embracing self-reliance requires a sprawling rural property and a lifetime of experience. This is simply not true. Urban homesteading is a growing culture. Even apartment dwellers can incorporate significant changes towards more self-reliance into their lives. A small herb garden on a windowsill can supply fresh ingredients for cooking, while composting food scraps reduces waste and creates valuable fertilizer. Hanging laundry on the line or a drying rack and learning basic sewing skills for clothing re- pairs will extend the life of your wardrobe and reducing textile waste.

Let's look at some real-world examples. I know a young professional who lives in a tiny city apartment. She grows micro-greens and herbs in mason jars on her balcony. She composts in a small countertop composter and makes her own cleaning solutions. Is she entirely self-sufficient? No, but she's made significantly important changes and feels a greater sense of control over her life. What's next for her? From her phone calls to me sourdough making is a good possibility. Not only will she benefit from the health aspects of sourdough but it will save on her grocery bill.

There's is a delightful family I know in the suburbs who trans- formed a small patch of their yard into a productive vegetable garden. I may have pestered them into it a bit. Or maybe I inspired them, there's no telling. They learned how to grow those vegetables from seeds and how to preserve their harvest through canning and freezing. Now, they will be providing nutritious meals for their family throughout the year. I remember when they grew their first strawberry and picked their first batch of green bean. Their excitement overwhelmed me!

They also embraced DIY projects by repairing household items and building their own fire pit instead of purchasing a pre-made one. These steps reduced their reliance on costly items and repairs. They found joy in the process. With the kids pitching in, they are strengthening their family bonds while decreasing their environ- mental impact. These are just a few examples of the many ways individuals are incorporating self-reliance into their daily lives.

The key is to start small. Set realistic goals and gradually building your skill set. What interests you most? You don't have to be perfect at every task or be an expert in area of self-sufficiency. Try not to allow yourself to become overwhelmed by the enormity of the task. Although I admit, it happens to all of us at one time or another.

Focus on one area at a time. Do you want to learn to compost your kitchen scraps? Master this one single skill before moving onto the next. Perhaps you can begin with learning how to make your own bread, then move on to growing a few herbs. After that, maybe learn how to tackle basic home repairs. Each small success builds confidence making the journey more enjoyable and fulfilling.

I will admit I am not as young as I used to be (lets not tell my husband I said that). I wish I had truly dedicated myself to being more self-sufficient 20 years ago. I have to face the fact that my brain is no longer that young sponge ready to soak up every bit of information it comes across. But I continue to learn new techniques and ideas by taking it one step at a time. My advice to you is embrace the learning process.

There are countless resources available, from online tutorials and books, like this one, to local workshops and community gardens. Connect with other self-reliant individuals. Believe me, we love sharing knowledge, experiences, and providing mutual support.

Remember that self-reliance is not a competitive sport. We learn from each other and inspire one another.
The modern world throws many challenges our way, economic in-stability, environmental concerns, and the ever present feeling of just being overwhelmed with the demands of life. But by embracing a more self-sufficient lifestyle, you are not just preparing for these challenges, you are equipping yourself to thrive though them.

You are fostering resilience, not only in your personal life but also within your community. You're creating a more sustainable and fulfilling existence for yourself and your family.
So, are you ready to get started on this journey? Let's begin by assessing your current level of self-sufficiency. Together we will identify areas for growth, and craft a personalized plan that fits your unique circumstances.

Remember, even small steps can lead to significant, lasting changes. Let's build those strong roots, together.

Setting Realistic Goals

Kari Pouli

Now that we've taken stock of our current skills and understand areas for growth, it's time to turn those aspirations into a concrete plan. The key here is to set realistic goals.

Forget the fantastical vision of achieving complete self-sufficiency overnight. It doesn't exist. That's a recipe for burnout and disappointment. Instead, let's embrace a more sustainable, step-by-step approach. Look at it as building a sturdy house, brick by brick, rather than attempting to magically poof it into existence with a wave of a magic wand.

The first step is to realize your priorities. What aspects of self-reliance are most important to you? Is it growing your own food? Mastering basic home repairs? Reducing your dependence on plastic?

Perhaps it's a combination of several factors. What is most important to me may not be the same for you. Realizing your priorities allows you to focus your energy and resources effectively. Don't try to tackle everything at once! Choose a few key areas and get to work.

Once you've identified what is most important to you, it's time to set SMART goals. SMART stands for Specific, Measurable, Achievable, Relevant, and Time-bound. Let's break this down:

Specific: Avoid vague goals like "I'm going to eat healthier." In- stead, try for something specific, like "I will grow five tomato plants and harvest at least ten pounds of tomatoes by the end of August." The more specific your goal, the easier it will be to track your progress and stay motivated.

Measurable: How will you measure your success? As with the tomato example, the measurable aspect is the ten pounds of tomatoes. For other goals, it might be the number of items you've re- paired, the amount of waste you've reduced, or the number of hours you have spent learning a new skill. When you have measurable targets, it provides tangible evidence of your progress. Let's face it, when a goal is reached, you will gain more confidence and be encouraged to continue your journey.

Achievable: Set goals that are challenging but attainable within your current circumstances. Don't set yourself up for failure by aiming too high too soon. You cannot raise milk cows when you live in a city apartment and don't own any land. Start small. Then take the time to celebrate each of your successes. Slowly increase the difficulty of your goals as you gain experience and confidence

Relevant: Ensure that your goals align with your overall desires and lifestyle. If you live in a small apartment with limited sunlight, aiming to grow a sprawling vegetable garden might be unrealistic. Instead, focus on container gardening or growing herbs indoors with a hydroponic system. Relevance keeps you focused and prevents you from wasting time and energy on goals that aren't realis- tic in your current situation

Time-bound: Set a deadline for achieving your goals. This adds a sense of urgency and accountability. Instead of trying to "learn to can," try "learn to can tomatoes and peaches by the end of my birthday." Having a deadline encourages you to stay on track and prevents your goals from becoming a flat tire and stranding you where you stand.

Let's look at some examples of SMART goals across different areas of self-reliance:

Food Production and Preservation:

Instead of: "Improve my cooking skills."
Try: "Learn three new recipes using seasonal vegetables and prepare one of these recipes twice a week for the next two months." *Instead of:* "Grow more vegetables."
Try: "Plant five pepper plants in my garden and harvest at least 20 peppers by October."
Instead of: "Preserve some of my harvest."
Try: "Can ten jars of tomatoes and five jars of peaches by the end of September, using a water bath canner."

Household Maintenance and Repairs:

Instead of: "Fix things around the house."
Try: "Learn how to replace a leaky faucet and replace the one in my bathroom by the end of next month."
Instead of: "Reduce my reliance on store-bought cleaning sup- plies."
Try: "Make my own all-purpose cleaner using vinegar and essential oils and use it exclusively for the next three months." *Instead of:* "Save energy."
Try: "Switch to LED light bulbs throughout the house and reduce my monthly energy consumption by 10% within two months."

Resource Management:

Instead of: "Reduce waste."
Try: "Reduce my weekly trash by 25% by composting food scraps and actively seeking recyclable options for packaging."

Instead of: "Conserve water."
Try: "Install low-flow showerheads and reduce my daily water us- age by 15 gallons within one month."

Instead of: "Improve my finances."
Try: "Create a detailed monthly budget and track my spending for the next three months and save 10% of my income each month."

Essential Skills and Knowledge:

Instead of: "Learn first aid."
Try: "Complete a certified first aid and CPR course by the end of June."
Instead of: "Do basic car maintenance."
Try: "Learn how to change a tire, check my oil level, and do this every month during the next three months."
Instead of: "Improve my digital literacy."
Try: "Take an online course on effective online research techniques and complete it within one month."

These are just examples. You should tailor your goals to your individual circumstances. The key is to break down larger goals into smaller and manageable steps. Don't be afraid to adjust your goals as you learn and grow.

Life throws curve balls all the time. Life happens! Things come up. But flexibility is key. Don't get discouraged if you fall behind schedule. Simply reassess your plan and adjust accordingly. The important thing is to keep moving forward, even if it's slow and steady.

Building a self-reliant lifestyle is a journey. Each day, month, and year you grow, change, and progress. Embrace the process, celebrate your small victories, and don't be afraid to ask for help when needed.

There's a large community of self-sufficient enthusiasts and homesteaders out there! They want to share their knowledge and support your journey. Connect with them, learn from their experiences, and share your own triumphs and challenges. And who knows, you might even find yourself inspiring others along the way!

Assessing You Current Level of Self-Sufficiency

Before we dive headfirst into the exciting and let's be honest, slightly terrifying, world of self-reliance, let's take a moment to catch our breath and take a look at the lay of the land. Understanding your starting point is necessary to create a plan that will lead you to successfully claim your independence.

This isn't about judging your current abilities (or lack thereof). It's about accepting and using your unique quirks to forge a path to personal success. So, think of it as a starting point on a journey where we will face challenges head-on and celebrate even the tiniest victories! This isn't about judging your current abilities (or lack thereof). It's about accepting and using your unique quirks to forge a path to personal success. So, think of it as a starting point on a journey where we will face challenges head-on and celebrate even the tiniest victories!

Now, let's talk more about you. Take a good look at where you are right now. Are you standing at the base of the mountain and gearing up for the climb? Or perhaps you're already halfway up, pausing to admire the view and catching your breath. Maybe you're that adventurous person who's already reached the summit once and is now getting ready for an even taller peak.

Wherever you are, it's essential to know because it's your unique starting point. It's from here that you'll measure how far you've come and the incredible progress you'll make.

This journey is all about embracing your true, authentic self and letting go of any self-doubt or limitations you think you may have.

So, take a deep breath, and let's begin. Together, we'll navigate the twists and turns, overcome obstacles, and celebrate the small wins leading to a life of self-reliance and pure awesomeness!

There is a saying lets "get down to brass tacks." This self-assessment isn't about comparing yourself to some mythical, perfectly self-sufficient homesteader, because those folks mainly exist in fantasy novels! Instead, we're focusing on practical skills and knowledge relevant to daily life.

At this point, the aim is to identify your strengths and the areas where you can build greater skills. So, grab some paper and something to write with so you can answer with the utmost honesty.

Let's begin with an honest review of your skills in several key areas:

1. Food Preparation:

Gardening: Do you currently grow any food? If so, what? Herbs on a windowsill? A large vegetable patch? A sprawling orchard? Be honest about the scale and success of your gardening experience. Consider the challenges you've faced, like pests, diseases, limited space, and how you've overcome them. For me, it's vine borers! If you currently do not have a garden, consider what's preventing you from starting one. Is it the lack of space, knowledge, or time.

Cooking from Scratch: How much of your food is prepared from scratch versus per-packaged or takeout? Are you comfortable with basic cooking techniques like roasting, sautéing, and braising? Can you bake bread? Do you feel confident in improving recipes or adapting them to the ingredients you have on hand? Honestly assess your comfort level with different cooking methods and ingredients.

Food Preservation: Do you preserve any food? Are you familiar with canning, freezing, drying, or fermenting? These methods ex- tend the shelf life of your harvest and reduce reliance on store-bought items. Even simple methods like freezing extra produce can significantly enhance your level of self-sufficiency. Think about your experience with food preservation techniques. Discover what you already know and what you'd like to learn.

2. Household Maintenance and Repairs:

Basic Repairs: Can you perform simple home repairs? Patch a hole in the wall? Fix a leaky faucet? Mend clothes? These seemingly small skills can save you a considerable amount of money and reduce your dependence on outside services. Consider the tools you own and your competency in using them. Apparently, I am not "allowed" to use the circular saw... anymore—long story.

Cleaning and Maintenance: Do you make your own cleaning products or rely on commercially available ones? Consider the environmental impact and potential health consequences of your choices. Your choices may have an environmental impact and potential health consequences. If you aren't willing to make your own cleaning products, consider purchasing chemical-free and environ- mentally friendly products on the market for a greener approach.

Energy Conservation: Are you aware of your energy consumption? Do you take steps to conserve energy at home? Energy independence is a significant aspect of self-sustainability. Explore areas where you can reduce your energy footprint, from adding solar power options to using energy-efficient appliances, to practicing simple habits like turning off lights.

3. Resource Management:

Waste Reduction: How efficiently do you manage your household waste? Do you recycle, compost, or find ways to reuse items?

Reducing waste is a major step towards a sustainable lifestyle. Think carefully about your current waste management practices and areas for improvement.

Water Conservation: Are you conscious of your water usage? Do you take steps to conserve water in your daily routines? Do you run the water while brushing your teeth? Water is a precious re- source, and self-reliance involves managing it wisely. Reflect on your current water consumption habits and find ways to use less.

Financial Management: How effectively do you manage your finances? Financial independence forms the foundation of true self-sufficiency. It allows you to make independent choices and make it through those unexpected events. Assess your financial practices to ensure you build a solid foundation for long-term independence.

4. Essential Skills and Knowledge:

First Aid and Basic Healthcare: Do you have basic first-aid skills? Are you CPR certified? Do you know anything about herbalism? Knowing how to handle minor injuries and illnesses can prevent unnecessary trips to the doctor and increase your preparedness. Consider expanding your first aid knowledge by taking a course or reviewing relevant resources.

Basic Car Maintenance: Can you perform basic car maintenance tasks, like checking tire pressure or changing a tire? While not everyone is a mechanic, and I can attest that I am not. However, knowledge of basic car maintenance skills can prevent unexpected breakdowns and reduce reliance on roadside assistance.

Digital Literacy and Information Access: Access to reliable information is crucial in the modern age. Assess your digital literacy and your ability to find credible and accurate information online. Developing the ability to perform online research effectively is essential for continuing learning and personal development.

Now, let's move beyond the checklist. Finally, right?

Remember, it's not about what you know, it's about what you are willing to learn. This is your journey, and it's extremely personal. Consider the following questions to refine your self-assessment further:

What are your biggest challenges in achieving greater self-reliance? Be honest about the obstacles you face. Is it limited space, lack of time, financial constraints, or simply a lack of confidence?

What are your biggest motivators for pursuing a self-reliant lifestyle? Identifying your reasons. Are you looking for financial freedom? Do you have health concerns with today's food production, or is it about environmental consciousness? Maybe it's simply a desire for greater independence. What will fuel your progress and keep you motivated?

What small steps can you take today to increase your self-sufficiency? Start with one manageable goal. Perhaps it's starting a small herb garden, learning a basic repair technique, or committing to cooking one meal from scratch each week.

What resources are available to you? Consider local community gardens, workshops, online courses, libraries, and fellow enthusiasts who can offer support and guidance.

This isn't a right or wrong test. It's a personal inventory—an opportunity to reflect on your strengths and look at areas for improvement.

The process of honest self-assessment is the foundation on which you'll build your personalized path toward a more self-reliant and fulfilling life. Remember that every small step forward will bring you closer to a larger, more meaningful journey.

Don't get discouraged by perceived shortcomings; embrace the learning process and celebrate each small victory along the way. And always remember, you're not alone on this path. We are learning together.

Essential Tools and Resources

iStock

Now that we've laid the groundwork for setting realistic goals, let's start with the practical aspects of building your self-reliant toolkit. Gathering the right tools and re- sources is essential for success, but it should not require a huge upfront investment or a complete overhaul of your life. Remember, we're building a foundation, brick by brick.

So, let's start with the basics. Think of this as a wish list. Don't feel pressured to get everything at once. Prioritize what you think you will need based on your SMART goals.

I. Kitchen Essentials: The Heart of Self-Sustenance

A well-equipped kitchen is the basis of self-sufficient living. It's where we transform raw ingredients into nourishing meals.

It is where we preserve our harvest and reduce our reliance on processed foods. While a top-of-the-line chef's knife set might be tempting, and for me, it definitely is, it is not necessary right now.

Let's focus on practical, versatile tools.

Good quality chef's knife: A single, sharp chef's knife (8-10 inches) is worth far more than a set of eight. Learn to sharpen it properly. It's an investment that will pay off in the long run. I can tell you from experience, and a whole lot of sliced fingers, there are far fewer accidents when you have a good knife. You can find excellent knives at reasonable prices; look for brands known for their durability and sharpness.

Cutting board: Go for a sturdy, non-porous cutting board. I prefer wood. Avoid glass, as it can dull your knives quickly. Try having two cutting boards, one for produce and one for meat. This will help avoid cross-contamination from raw meat to vegetables.

Mixing bowls: A set of three or four mixing bowls in different sizes will handle most tasks. Stainless steel is durable and easy to clean. However, well-made glass or ceramic bowls are also great options.

Measuring cups and spoons: Accurate measurement is crucial for cooking and baking. Invest in a reliable set. I use a stainless-steel set.

Canning equipment: If you are going to preserve what you grow, this is a priority. You will need a canner. A water bath canner is more affordable, but a pressure canner can be multi-functional for both water bath and pressure canning. You will need jars with lids and rings, as well as a jar lifter. Again, there are so many lids to choose from. I would not suggest using reusable lids until you have gained some experience canning. Honestly, there are hundreds of free online resources, not to mention books, that provide detailed instructions for healthy, safe canning techniques. Do your home- work with this. Food safety is non-negotiable.

Basic cookware: A good quality saucepan, frying pan, and baking sheet are essential. Cast iron is a fantastic investment. It's incredibly durable and distributes heat evenly. But it requires seasoning and a bit of care. If learning to season and clean cast iron seems daunting, high-quality stainless steel cookware is an excellent alternative.

Food processor or blender (optional but helpful): These appliances speed up food preparation. A food processor can chop, slice, and dice, while a blender is perfect for smoothies, soups, and sauces. If your budget is tight, prioritize one over the other based on your kitchen needs.

Hand-crank grinder (optional): I have to say this piece of equipment changed my life. Not really, but there is nothing better than homemade sausage! A hand-crank grinder allows you to grind your own meat, grains, and spices, increasing your self-sufficiency and offering a satisfying tactile experience.

II. Gardening Tools: Growing Your Own Food

Providing homegrown food for your family offers a deep connection to the earth as you gain incredible satisfaction. Even if you have limited space, container gardening or vertical gardening can be incredibly productive. You will need:

Gardening gloves: Protect your hands from dirt, thorns, and other irritants.

Trowel and hand rake: These are perfect for small-scale gardening and container gardening.

Watering can or hose: Choose the option most convenient for your setup. If using a hose, a nozzle with various spray settings offers flexibility.

Shovel and spade (for larger gardens): These are necessary if you're working with a larger garden plot.

Gardening tools such as rake, pruning shears, and a hoe: These tools are crucial for maintaining your garden and performing tasks like pruning, weeding, and tilling. Invest in quality tools that will last.

Seed starting supplies: If you're starting seeds indoors, you'll need seed trays, seed starting mix, and grow lights, especially important during the winter months. I do need to add that part of a self-sufficient lifestyle is repurposing materials. Do you have a used butter container? Add holes in the bottom and soil. An empty paper towel roll? Just cut it into two-inch pieces and fill it with soil. These items can be used for seed starting without spending money on needless trays.

III. Household Maintenance and Repair Tools:

A few basic tools can go a long way in maintaining your home and preventing small problems from becoming bigger ones.

Screwdrivers (Phillips and Flathead): A set of both types in various sizes is a must.

Hammer: Choose a claw hammer for versatility.

Pliers (needle-nose and slip-joint): These are helpful for a variety of tasks.

Tape measure: A reliable tape measure is crucial for any DIY project.

Level: Being sure things are level is important for all types of home improvement tasks.

Wrench set: A small set of wrenches can save you from countless frustrating situations. Again, I know from experience.

Utility knife: A sharp utility knife is versatile. You never know when you need a sharp edge.

IV. First Aid and Emergency Preparedness:

Having a well-stocked first-aid kit and emergency supplies is vital to self-reliance. There is peace in knowing you can handle minor injuries and unexpected events. Comprehensive first-aid kit: This is a no-brainier for me. A comprehensive first-aid kit should contain bandages, antiseptic wipes, pain relievers, antibiotic ointment, and other essential supplies.

Emergency food and water supply: Store a supply of non-perishable food and water that will last for at least 72 hours.

Flashlight and extra batteries: Reliable lighting is imperative during power outages.

Portable radio: Stay informed during emergencies by having a portable radio that can receive weather alerts and other important broadcasts.

V. Sourcing Materials Sustainably and Ethically:

While convenience might tempt you towards mass-produced tools, prioritize sourcing your materials sustainably and ethically.

Used tools: Check online marketplaces, garage sales, and thrift stores for used tools. You can often find excellent quality tools at a fraction of the cost. This is a great way to reduce your environmental impact and save some money.

Supporting local businesses: Whenever possible, support your lo- cal hardware stores and businesses that value sustainable practices. This will strengthen your local community and support businesses that share your values.

Repairing and re-purposing: Learn basic repair skills. A simple repair can extend a tool's or an item's life and reduce waste. Re-purposing items for other purposes also contribute to reducing your environmental impact.

DIY solutions: Many items can be made at home using readily available materials. For example, you can make your own cleaning solutions using vinegar and essential oils, reducing your dependency on chemical-filled products.

Remember, start with the basics: Focus on what supports your priorities and SMART goals. Gradually expand your toolkit as you gain experience and confidence. Embrace the learning process and ask for help when needed. In the end, the satisfaction of creating a more self-sufficient life is truly rewarding.

Overcoming Challenges and Obstacles

There will always be challenges that will pop up on our journey towards self-reliance. Unfortunately, this isn't a fairy tale that we can just step into, and voila, it is an easy and peaceful lifestyle. This changes a real-life choice, and it comes complete with its share of bumps in the road. But rest assured, your obstacles can be overcome, and the lessons you learn along the way will be invaluable.

One of the biggest concerns in homesteading and self-sufficient living is limited space. Many of you live in apartments, condos, or small houses with little to no backyard space.

Look really closely at your surroundings. You can even transform a sunny windowsill into a productive little garden patch. Remember, it's about making the most of the space you have, not wishing for the space you don't have.

Another common challenge is time constraints. Finding the time to dedicate yourself to self-reliant pursuits can feel overwhelming between work, family, and other commitments. The key here is to approach self-reliance gradually and strategically. Again, start small! It's hard to take things slow when you are "all in." Instead of aiming for complete self-sufficiency overnight, build your skills and knowledge over time, or you will wind up burned out.

Financial limitations are another significant obstacle many of us deal with. Investing in tools, seeds, and other resources can seem worrying, particularly when budgets are tight.

However, self-reliance isn't necessarily about expensive equipment or high-end bougie ingredients. Smart shopping, DIY projects, and being resourceful can go a long way. Think out of the box!

You may feel that you cannot embrace this way of life. The image of a sprawling homestead with acres of land dedicated to gardening and livestock is a romantic ideal. And honestly, it is a dream of mine. But it is not a requirement. Believe it or not, a great deal can be achieved in small spaces.

Let's take a look at vertical gardening. In my book "*Urban Homesteading for Beginners: Starting Where You Are.*" I go into detail on vertical gardening. There are so many options, from towering planters and hanging baskets to stacked containers, that can maximize your growing area without taking up valuable floor space.

Look into compact fruit trees or dwarf varieties and plant them in barrel containers. Fill in around the trunk with short, rooted fruit like strawberries or vegetables like lettuce. And don't forget the balcony. It's often unused space.

You could use grow lights to supplement natural sunlight and take up indoor gardening with a small hydroponic system. These systems produce good yields in a relatively small area. I actually prefer to grow my lettuce indoors rather than in outdoor containers since it is protected from temperature changes, dirt, and insects.

Consider buying used tools, re-purposing items, and borrowing or sharing resources with friends or neighbors. A freeze dryer is on my wish list, but my bank account believes we need milk more. So, what did I do? I found someone I knew who owned one and asked if she would consider freeze-drying some of my harvest. In exchange, I give her a portion. Looking for land? Many community gardens offer plots for a small fee.

Start with low-cost or free seeds, which can often be found through seed swaps or from friends and family.

Learn to repair rather than replace. Look for low-cost or free re sources online and at your local library.

Learning to preserve your harvest keeps you from buying already processed and, may I say, unhealthy foods, significantly impacting your grocery budget over time. Even the simplest preserving methods, like freezing and dehydrating, can make a huge difference.

Then there's the challenge of a lack of knowledge and experience. Did you start your life knowing how to walk, talk, or even feed yourself?

Most of us don't start life or our self-reliant journey as seasoned experts. We learn along the way. We make mistakes. And that's perfectly okay. The beauty of self-reliance is that it's a journey of constant learning and discovery.

Take advantage of online resources like YouTube tutorials, blogs, and online forums. Join a local community gardening club or workshops to learn from experienced gardeners and homesteaders.

Don't hesitate to ask questions. Most people in the homesteading community are more than happy to share their knowledge. In fact, we love to talk about sourdough. Books like what you are reading now provide structured guidance. Remember, there is no shame in asking for help and learning from others' mistakes. Each challenge is a stepping stone toward greater knowledge and skill.

Unexpected setbacks will always be a part of your journey. A failed crop, a broken tool, a sudden illness, it happens. Do you give up? Throw in the towel? No! The solution is to develop resilience and problem-solving skills. Don't let setbacks discourage you from the lifestyle you dream of.

Look at what went wrong, figure out how you can do better, and try again. Keep a detailed garden journal and document your successes and failures.

This will help you learn from each experience. Self-reliance isn't about avoiding problems; it's about equipping yourself to handle them effectively.

Finally, a common pitfall is becoming overwhelmed. This lifestyle can be an incredibly inspiring experience, but it's also easy to get overwhelmed by the sheer number of skills and tasks involved.

Break down large projects into smaller and more manageable steps. Instead of aiming to build a chicken coop from scratch
immediately, start with building a simple raised garden bed. Focus on mastering one skill at a time and allow yourself to grow at your own pace.

Above all, do not compare your progress to others. Your journey is unique and personal. There is no one-size-fits-all path to
self-reliance.

Becoming more self-sufficient is deeply personal and rewarding. It's about feeling empowered, being resilient, and connecting to something larger than ourselves. It celebrates the past. Remember, even small acts of self-sufficiency contribute to a more resilient and fulfilling life. So, take a deep breath, embrace the process, and, above all, enjoy the ride.

Two

The Self-Sufficient Kitchen

Mastering Basic Cooking Techniques

Pexels

The self-sufficient kitchen is a place where creativity and culinary magic collide. After avoiding the traps of toxic takeout and embracing our inner resourcefulness, it's time to venture into the heart of our culinary domain and unleash the power of...duh duh duh basic cooking techniques.

Forget fancy culinary dishes and complicated recipes. This is about building a solid foundation of practical and adaptable skills. We are going back to the basics of my friends! We are building skills that will make our homegrown harvests sing and our taste buds dance with delight! Okay, I know that sounded cheesy. Roll up your sleeves, grab your aprons, yes, I use aprons, and get ready to master your self-sufficient kitchen.

The beauty of self-sufficient cooking lies in its simplicity. It's about self-sufficiency, resourcefulness, and reconnecting with
traditional skills that allow us to live more sustainably. Learning homesteading skills doesn't just save money; it also fosters independence and a deeper appreciation for the food and products we use daily.

We're not aiming for Michelin-star meals (I would rather have a plate of fluffy biscuits and gravy) but rather for wholesome and satisfying dishes made with ingredients you've either grown your- self or sourced locally. This approach reduces your reliance on chemical-filled processed foods, lowers your environmental impact, and connects you more deeply to the food you consume.

If you want a practical kitchen, you will need to keep it stocked with the basics. I'm talking flour, yeast, sugar, salt, rice, and beans. Of course, if you don't eat rice, then don't stock it! This is your kitchen.

Customize it for what you and your family eat. How about longer-lasting perishables like potatoes, onions, and squash? Do you keep them on hand or run to the supermarket at the last minute?

Then there's dairy like milk, yogurt, butter, cheese, and sour cream. Is it part of your goals to make your own, or will you continue to purchase these items? An organized kitchen will be incredibly helpful. So, if you are already an incredible cook and a master in the kitchen, you can skip this section.

Let's start with cooking basics: mastering the art of **boiling**. Seems simple, right? Now I am not trying to insult you. But there's more to it than just tossing something into a pot of water.

Boiling is the foundation for many dishes, from perfectly cooked pasta to tender vegetables. The key is to use enough water to sub- merge the ingredients properly and to bring the water to a rolling boil before adding them. This ensures even cooking and prevents sticking.

Did you know that a perfectly boiled egg starts with room temperature water? The egg is added, then once the water comes to a boil, the time should be set for six to eight minutes, depending on how well-done you like your yolk cooked. Aim for al dente, firm but tender, rather than mushy, for vegetables. Your family will most likely enjoy them more. Overcooked vegetables not only lack flavor and texture but also lose valuable nutrients. You don't want to go through all the hard work of growing your own vegetables only to overcook them into a sloppy mess.

Try experimenting with different boiling times to find what works best for your liking and the specific vegetables. Don't forget the power of adding a pinch of salt to the boiling water. It enhances the flavor and helps maintain the color of your vegetables.

Next, there is **roasting**. Roasting is a fantastic way to bring out the natural sweetness and depth of flavor in vegetables and meats. The key is high heat and good space in the pan or baking dish. If it is overcrowded, it will lead to steaming instead of roasting, and again, soggy vegetables instead of beautifully browned and caramelized ones. A little bit of olive oil, salt, and pepper are
usually all you need—let the natural flavors shine.

Use the herbs you grow. Experiment with your roasted vegetables and meat. Rosemary and garlic pair wonderfully with potatoes, while thyme complements root vegetables.

For roasting meats, pre-heating your oven is essential for a good outer crust. Baste your meat regularly during roasting to keep it moist and flavorful. A meat thermometer is your best friend. Be sure it reaches the proper internal temperature before serving.

Sautéing is another excellent technique for quickly cooking vegetables and creating flavorful sauces. Use a good-quality pan—I love stainless steel or cast iron—and oil with a high smoke point.

Coconut oil and tallow are great and healthy choices. Work in batches to avoid overcrowding the pan. If you use a higher heat you can give your vegetables a nice sear, creating beautiful color and enhancing the flavor.

With sautéing, timing is crucial. Follow the directions. Mastering the art of sautéing allows you to create quick and healthy week- night meals.

Let's not forget **baking**. There is nothing better than walking into a house with the decadent smell of baking bread or pastries. But don't limit baking to just desserts or bread. It's a fantastic way to cook vegetables and make delicious casseroles with your leftovers.

When it comes to baking bread and other baked goods, accurate measurements and proper mixing techniques are important for success. Follow the recipe. Baking is a science. Each ingredient is purposely set to trigger the desired result.

Once you are confident in your baking skills, don't be afraid to experiment with different flours or add-ins, such as oats or nuts, to enhance flavor and texture. Many recipes can be easily adapted to reflect your own tastes and available ingredients once you master the basics.

Steaming is a gentle cooking method that retains nutrients and produces beautifully tender vegetables. I love picking fresh green beans from the garden and steaming them for dinner. If you do not have a designated stovetop steamer, then you could use a steamer basket over a pot of boiling water.

I prefer the steamer. Just plug it in and go. Steaming is perfect for delicate vegetables like asparagus, broccoli, or peas that can quickly become overcooked with other methods. To successfully steam them, make sure the vegetables are laid out evenly in the steamer basket, allowing the steam to circulate freely.

Now, let's explore **braising**. Braising combines browning, simmering and slow cooking, resulting in incredibly tender and flavorful meats. First, you begin by browning the meat in a super-hot pan to create a crisp crust. Then you transfer the meat to a Dutch oven or other heavy-bottomed pot with liquid, like broth or wine, add vegetables, and simmer until tender. Braising is a perfect method for tougher, less expensive cuts of meat. It turns the meat into melt-in- your-mouth deliciousness.

Mastering these basic cooking techniques is not about achieving culinary perfection but about building a strong foundation of practical kitchen skills. Understanding the principles of heat transfer, timing, and ingredient interaction will lead to mealtime success.

Don't be afraid to put your own originality into your meals. Cooking is a creative process; it's supposed to be enjoyable. Adapting from fast food to home cooking may take time, but your health and your family's health are worth the effort.

Minimizing your food waste is another crucial aspect of self-sufficiency cooking. Your kitchen garden may yield a surplus of zucchini one year and a bumper crop of tomatoes next. The recipes you use should reflect the abundance of your harvest.

Plan your meals around what you have on hand, and be creative with leftovers. Part of self-sufficiency is doing our best not to waste.

Vegetable scraps can be frozen and later used to make flavorful stocks. Leftover veggies can be incorporated into fritters or salads. Of course, you can always compost. Composting food scraps will enrich your garden soil, creating a truly cyclical system.

Remember that there are no kitchen failures. Every burnt dish is a lesson learned, and every perfectly roasted vegetable is a testament to your growing skills. The self-sufficient kitchen is a journey of discovery, and the rewards are delicious and deeply fulfilling.

Preserving Your Harvest: Canning and Freezing

Now that we have learned about fundamental cooking techniques, let's turn our attention to preserving the fruits and vegetables of our labor or those purchased from the farmer's market. Preserving your harvest is necessary for extending the life of your homegrown bounty and ensuring you have nutritious food available all year round.

While some people may imagine cellars filled with jars and freezers overflowing with produce, the truth is that preserving can be adapted to suit any size space. For me and my family, I like to have prepared meals at the touch of my fingers. So, I have a lot of jars on the shelves filled with ready-to-go ingredients and pre-made meals like sausage and peppers.

Don't look at it like you're creating a commercial-scale operation. It can be six jars or a hundred. The goal is to extend the life of your hard work and ensure you can enjoy the taste of summer throughout the winter months.

There are two primary methods: canning and freezing. Canning, while requiring a bit more upfront investment in equipment, provides shelf-stable food that will last for years. Freezing, on the other hand, is quick and easy. It's ideal for preserving produce that does not can well, like berries or leafy greens. Both methods are valuable in a self-sufficient kitchen

Let's start with canning. Before diving into preserving specifics, I need to address food safety. Improper canning can lead to botulism, a serious and potentially fatal form of food poisoning.

Therefore, meticulous attention to detail and adherence to safe practices are extremely important. Always use up-to-date, reliable recipes and follow the instructions.

There are two primary methods of canning: water bath canning and pressure canning. Water bath canning is used for high-acid foods like jams, jellies, pickles, and fruits with a naturally high acid con- tent.

Pressure canning, on the other hand, is required for low-acid foods like vegetables, meats, and soups. These require a higher temperature to destroy potentially harmful bacteria, which the pressure cooker provides.

Let's break down the water bath canning process. You will require a few pieces of equipment.

First, you should have a large pot to boil water. It should be deep enough to cover your jars entirely with water, and a jar lifter for safely handling hot jars, canning jars, and lids. Always use new lids. Just one previously used lid with a dent can ruin the whole jar of food. I find that a wide-mouth funnel makes it easier to fill jars, and a bubble remover tool to eliminate air pockets. It can even be a chopstick.

Begin by sterilize your jars and lids. You can do this by washing the jars in hot, soapy water, then placing them in a boiling water bath for at least 10 minutes. Or the most modern method is running the jars through the dishwasher on the sanitize cycle. I clean out my jars and store them, then when it's time to can, I prefer to run the jars on sanitize through the dishwasher.

Back to the instructions! While the jars are sterilizing, prepare your recipe. Follow your chosen recipe exactly, ensuring accurate measurements and proper cooking times.

Once your recipe is ready, carefully ladle the hot mixture into the sterilized jars. Depending on the recipe, you will need to leave about ½ inch of headspace at the top. Use the bubble remover to remove any trapped air bubbles.

Wipe the rims of the jars clean with a damp cloth, then place the lids and screw the bands on tightly.

Next, carefully lower the jars into your boiling water bath. Be sure they are completely submerged in the water. Bring the water back to a rolling boil and process according to your recipe's instructions.

Following the correct processing time is crucial for achieving a proper seal and ensuring food safety. Once the processing time is complete, carefully remove the jars using the jar lifter and let them cool completely on a towel-lined surface. You should hear a "pop" sound as the jars seal. Any jars that haven't sealed should be refrigerated and consumed promptly.

Pressure canning requires a pressure canner. Do not confuse this with a pressure cooker. It is not the same! A pressure canner maintains a specific temperature and pressure for low-acid foods. The process is similar to water bath canning, but the processing times are different and critical for safety. Always follow the manufacturer's instructions for operating your pressure canner.

Once your timer has gone off, leave the pot alone. Wait until the steam has completely stopped and the pressure has gone down.

Then, it is safe to remove the lid and the jars with the jar lifter. As with water-bath canned items, place the jars on a towel-lined counter. Allow all canned items to sit for 24 hours before removing the outer rings and storing them.

Now, let's discuss freezing. Freezing is a whole lot simpler than canning and requires fewer supplies. You'll need freezer-safe containers or bags. I use a food saver to keep out any excess air.

Wash and prepare your produce as directed in your recipe. For fruits, you may want to blanch them briefly in boiling water to de- activate enzymes that can affect texture and flavor, then quickly plunge them into ice water to stop the cooking process. You can also clean them in a water-vinegar solution. Blanching is often recommended for vegetables to preserve color and nutrients.

Once your produce is prepared, package it in containers and label them clearly with the contents and date. Freeze immediately. Be sure containers are tightly sealed to prevent freezer burn. I can tell you from experience that freezer-burned green beans are pretty gross. Properly frozen produce can generally be stored for several months, depending on the type of food.

Regardless of the preservation method you choose, always remember that proper food safety is essential. Use reliable recipes, clean your equipment thoroughly, and follow instructions carefully. If you have any doubts about the safety of your preserved food, it's always best to be cautious and discard it.

Above all, don't be intimidated by the process. With a bit of practice, you will be confidently preserving your homegrown food.

Here are a few simple recipes to get you started:

Michael Jarmoluk

Water Bath Canning: Strawberry Jam

This recipe uses a simple water bath canning method, which is great for beginners. You will need strawberries, sugar, lemon juice, and pectin. Pectin is a thickening agent that helps your jellies and jams reach the gel

stage. There are recipes that are pectin-free, and I encourage you to try them. But I found that this recipe is more user-friendly for first- time jam makers. The result will be a delicious, homemade jam that captures the summer sweetness.

Ingredients
4 pounds of whole strawberries
1 (1.75 ounce) package of low or no-sugar-needed powdered pectin
4 cups of granulated sugar, divided 2 tablespoons lemon juice

Instructions

Wash and hull the berries. Add them to a large bowl and crush them with a potato masher. Stir pectin and 1/4 cup of sugar into the berries.

Pour the crushed berries into a large, deep-sided saucepan or Dutch oven, and heat over medium-high heat, stirring constantly.

Bring the jam mixture to a boil, then add the remaining sugar. Stir continuously and boil hard for 1 minute.

Remove the jam from the heat and cool for 5 minutes. Skim off any foam.

Ladle the jam into hot, clean half-pint jars. Allowing 1/4-inch headspace. Use the bubble removing tool. Wipe the rims clean.

Place the lids and bands on each jar and adjust to fingertip tight. Place it in boiling water bath and process for 10 minutes. Remove from canner and allow to cool.

Pressure Canning: Green Beans

Jason Gillman

This recipe requires a pressure canner. You will need fresh green beans, salt, and water. Yup, that's it. I prefer to can green beans by the pint. However, if you double the recipe you can easily convert it to quarts. The result is a flavorful and nutritious side dish, ready to be enjoyed through- out the year.

Ingredients
1/2 lbs. cleaned green beans per pint jar approximately 1/2 tsp canning salt per pint jar
3/4 cups boiling water per pint jar

Instructions

Prepare your pressure canner according to the specified instructions.

Clean and cut the beans. Boil a pot of water.

Fill the sterilized jars about ⅓ full and gently tap the jar's bottom lightly to ensure the beans are well packed. Repeat for the remain- ing ⅔ of the jar, leaving ½-inch of headspace at the top.

Add the canning salt to each jar.

Pour boiling water over the prepared beans, leaving a ½-inch of headspace.
Wipe rims clean. Place lids and rings on jars and tighten until fin- ger-tight.

Pressure at 10 pounds for 20 minutes. For quart jars, 25 minutes. Set your timer. Watch the pressure throughout time and adjust the heat. The pressure needs to stay at 10 pounds of pressure.

After the timer goes off, remove from the heat and allow it to cool until the pressure gauge shows zero. You can adjust the time for your elevation according to the USDA canning guide, which you can find online.

Remove the jars from the canner and cool for 24 hours. Label and store your jars.

Freezing: Mixed Berries

This is an easy way to preserve the sweetness and color of summer berries.

Couleur

Soak berries in water and vinegar. By soaking your fruit, the tiny insects that like to take up residence in it will be forced to evict the premises.

Rinse and gently dry your berries.

Spread them out on a baking sheet with parchment paper or a sili cone mat.

Freeze berries. This will prevent the fruit from freezing into clumps. Place flash-frozen berries into freezer-safe bags or con- tainers. This is a great way to enjoy fresh berries in smoothies,
yogurt, or baked goods in the colder months.

There are several other ways to preserve your food, including de- hydrating, freeze-drying, smoking, and fermenting. Many tutorials are available. I have provided you with the basic top three. Feel free to explore what methods you prefer.

Preserving your harvest is rewarding. It connects you to your food, reduces your reliance on commercially produced foods, and allows you to savor the taste of summer fruit and vegetables long after the growing season has ended, reminding you of your summertime accomplishments.

Although food preservation requires some initial investment in equipment and time, the rewards far outweigh the effort. Remember to start small, choose methods appropriate to your space and resources, and share your successes along the way!

Each jar of perfectly preserved jam or perfectly frozen vegetable is a testament to your self-sufficiency.

Reducing Food Waste: Repurposed and Storage

CSU-Extension

Now let's tackle the often overlooked, aspect of reducing food waste. We went over what to do with leftovers and mindful shopping in our budget friendly kitchen. In the self-sufficient kitchen, every ingredient counts, and minimizing waste isn't just environmentally responsible, it's fiscally smart.

An unplanned shopping trip is a recipe for disaster for your wallet and your refrigerator. Impulse buying often leads to the back of the fridge wilting and rotting or becoming lost in a sea of ice crystals in the back of the freezer.

Other than keeping a well-organized shopping list, pay close attention to what you already have. Before heading out, do a quick inventory of your pantry and refrigerator. This simple step can prevent duplicate purchases and highlight items nearing their expiration dates, prompting you to incorporate them into your meal plan.

Keep in mind that seemingly insignificant scraps can be repurposed into flavorful additions to future meals. Take a look at vegetable scraps. We are talking about onion peels, carrot tops, celery ends, they are the foundation of flavorful homemade stocks and broth. Put them in a freezer bag and when it's full make a big pot of vegetable or bone broth.

Proper storage is the unsung hero in the battle against food waste. Many perfectly good pieces of fruit or vegetables have met an un- timely, moldy end due to improper storage.

Understanding how to store different foods correctly can extend their shelf life. For instance, certain fruits like bananas and avocados release ethylene gas, which can accelerate the ripening process of other fruits and vegetables stored nearby. Keep them separated!

As for leafy greens, they should be stored in airtight containers to maintain their freshness. Root vegetables thrive in cool, dark places, while herbs prefer a cool and slightly damp environment.

And let's not forget the environmental impact of reducing food waste. The resources used to produce, package, transport, and dis- pose of food are significant. By minimizing waste, you're not only saving money but also contributing to a more sustainable lifestyle.

Composting food scraps is a simple but effective way to reduce your environmental impact while enriching your garden soil. Even if you live in an apartment, a small countertop composter can easily handle your kitchen scraps.

Reducing food waste is not about following rigid rules, it's about adopting a mindful approach to food and cooking.

By embracing these strategies, you'll not only save money and re- sources, but you'll also unlock a whole new level of creativity in your self-sufficient kitchen. You will begin to foster a deeper connection with the food you eat and the planet that provides it.

Budget Friendly Meal Planning and Grocery Shopping

Budget-friendly meal planning isn't about depriving yourself. It's more about strategic planning and mindful consumption. Part of being more self-reliant is maximizing the value of your food dol- lars and minimizing waste. Think of it as a culinary adventure in resourcefulness. This is where we learn to be more creative and frugal.

Successful budget-friendly eating is meal planning. Before you think about grocery shopping, take the time to plan your meals for the week. This simple act can save you money and time later in the week. It will also reduce your food waste.

I hate going into the refrigerator only to realize that I had forgotten about an entire bag of lettuce that was pushed to the back of the shelf. The waste is bad enough, but having to remove and clean up the gloppy mess is not what I had in mind for the evening.

Consider your schedule, dietary needs, and what's currently in season. Seasonal produce is almost always cheaper and tastier than out of season items. Check your local farmers' markets and com- munity supported agriculture (CSA) programs for the freshest, most affordable options.

Okay, let's get back to planning your meals. Try to use some of the same ingredients across multiple dishes. For example, a roasted chicken can become the star of Sunday dinner, then be shredded and used in salads, soups, or sandwiches throughout the week. A large batch of rice can serve as a side dish one night and be added to soup or served with stir-fry for another meal.

Overripe bananas? Try blending them into smoothies or baking them into bread.

Don't overlook your leftovers, they are your friends. Embrace them! They can drastically reduce food waste and boost your budget.

Let's jump into some practical strategies for making the most of your ingredients. One of the most effective techniques is to embrace the "from-scratch" philosophy.

Making your own sauces, dressings, and condiments is not only significantly cheaper than buying premade versions, but it also allows you to control the ingredients and avoid unwanted additives, chemicals, and preservatives. A vinaigrette requires only olive oil, vinegar, and seasonings. It's all readily available at a fraction of the cost of store-bought dressings.

What about making homemade stocks and broths made from vegetable scraps and bones? A large batch can be made and canned, ready for you when you need it.

Another key to saving money is minimizing processed foods. I have to say it. Processed foods are so bad for you. They are loaded with sodium, sugar, unhealthy fats, chemicals, and preservatives, making them both costly and detrimental to your health. Focus on eating whole, unprocessed ingredients.

Fruits, fresh or home-canned vegetables, grains, legumes, and lean proteins. These are not only more nutritious but also significantly cheaper than processed poison we often grab in a hurry. It takes some getting used to, but once you develop a taste for clean ingredients, it's hard to go back.

Smart grocery shopping is another crucial part of budget-friendly eating. Before heading to the store, create a detailed shopping list based on your meal plan. Be sure to include any ingredients you may need to avoid taking an additional trip to the grocery store.

Sticking to your list is vital. Impulse purchases are the enemy of a self-sufficient and cost-conscious kitchen.

Using store apps, we compare prices between different stores and brands, taking advantage of sales and coupons. Don't be afraid to buy non-perishable items in bulk when it makes financial sense. Just remember to store them properly to prevent spoilage.

Prioritize staples over convenience foods. Staples like rice, beans, lentils, oats, and pasta are inexpensive and versatile and a great foundation of many budget friendly meals. Quinoa, farro and black beans, for instance, add flavor and texture to your meals offering a welcome change from the usual rice and baked beans.

I love seasonal shopping. When fruits and vegetables are in season, they are plentiful making them less expensive. This also allows you to maximize their freshness and nutritional value. It's also a great time to start food preservation. Embrace seasonal produce by incorporating them not only into your meal planning but into home preservation efforts.

Even if you aren't growing them yourself, summer tomatoes can always be used in salads, sauces, and even as a side dish with some olive oil and fresh basil. Buying in bulk can lead to canning sauces and salsa. Similarly, winter squashes offer a variety of dishes, from soups and stews to roasted side dishes. Remember, preserving is a skill that becomes more intuitive and rewarding over time.

Reducing food waste takes careful planning and well thought out storage techniques. Properly store your produce to maximize its shelf life.

Utilize leftovers, turning them into new dishes to avoid throwing anything away. Composting food scraps is another way to minimize waste and enrich your garden soil. This is not only financially responsible but environmentally beneficial as well.

Now, let's take a look at some sample meal plans and shopping lists that you can adapt to your needs and personal tastes. Remember, this is only a starting point. The key is to find what works for you.

You may find you prefer a weekly plan or prefer to plan monthly.

Sample Weekly Meal Plan:
Monday: Lentil soup with whole-wheat bread (using leftover bread from baking)
Tuesday: Chicken and vegetable stir-fry with brown rice (using leftover chicken from Sunday's roast)
Wednesday: Black bean burgers on whole-wheat buns with a side salad
Thursday: Pasta with marinara sauce and vegetables (using homemade sauce)
Friday: Tuna salad sandwiches on whole-wheat bread (using canned tuna)
Saturday: Homemade pizza with seasonal vegetables
Sunday: Roasted chicken with roasted root vegetables

Sample Shopping List:

Lentils
Chicken
Black beans
Whole wheat bread
Brown rice
Pasta
Canned
tuna
Vegetables (seasonal
selections)

Pixabay

Pizza dough ingredients (flour, yeast, etc.) Root vegetables (pota- toes, carrots, etc.) Olive oil
Spices
Canned tomatoes (for marinara sauce)

This shopping list has been made to be flexible. The specific vegetables and root vegetables will depend on your local farmers' market or grocery store's seasonal produce. The key is to select fresh and healthy ingredients that can be used in multiple dishes.

Remember, budget-friendly cooking doesn't have to be bland or boring. By planning your meals carefully and using leftovers creatively, you can create delicious, nutritious, and affordable meals that will nourish your body and your soul. It's a journey, not a race, and the rewards, both financial and culinary, are well worth the effort.

Embrace the process, experiment with new recipes and ingredients, and enjoy the delicious fruits and vegetables of your labor.

Your self-sufficient kitchen is not only a place of creativity but also a testament to your resourcefulness and commitment to a more sustainable and fulfilling life.

Three

Gardening for Self-Sufficiency

Getting the Most from Your Space

Anna Tarazevich

For a truly self-sufficient lifestyle growing your own food is the cornerstone of freedom from big farm and overpriced produce. Ur- ban dwellers can maximize their gardening yields in limited spaces by carefully planning and taking advantage of unconventional areas like rooftops and balconies. Forget the sprawling acres of vegetable patches. If you're living in the city or have a small space, don't worry!

You can still grow a lot of plants with smart planning and creativity.

Think beyond the usual garden plots and use every bit of space you have. Think vertical gardening, or perhaps you have access to a rooftop, a balcony, or you can even use your windowsills. The key is to carefully assess your space and get innovative with your gardening.

Once you've mapped out your available space, analyze the sun- light. Most vegetables thrive in at least six hours of direct sunlight daily. Observe your property throughout the day, noting where the sun shines brightest and at what time of day. This will dictate where you plant your sun-loving crops, such as tomatoes, peppers, and zucchini.

On the other hand, crops that tolerate shade, like lettuce, spinach, and kale, can be placed in less sunny areas.

Next, consider the soil. Healthy soil is the foundation of a thriving garden. Conduct soil tests yearly to determine the nutrient content and pH level. Adjust the soil as needed using compost, manure, or other organic amendments. Improving your soil will enhance nutrient uptake, resulting in healthier and more productive plants.

Don't forget about drainage. Soggy soil is a recipe for root rot. Amend heavy clay soils with organic matter to improve drainage and aeration. If you are putting in garden beds or containers, you will most likely purchase soil. Most commercial soils include the nutrients your plants will need.

With your space and soil assessed, it's time to choose your crops. My first piece of advice is do not plant anything you or your family won't eat. You are wasting valuable time, space and resources.

Focus on family favorite vegetables that offer high-yield and com- pact varieties. If you love watermelon, plant miniature versions.

Look for determinate tomato varieties, which will produce a larger yield over a shorter period.

Indeterminate varieties will continue growing and producing fruit over a longer season but will require a lot more space and without a guaranteed larger harvest.

Now here is where it starts to get exciting. It's time to select your gardening methods.

Vertical gardening is a fantastic solution for maximizing space. Think hanging baskets, trellises, and vertical planters. These techniques allow climbing plants like pole beans, cucumbers, and peas to grow vertically. It will free up ground space for other crops like carrots, beets, and lettuce. Vertical gardens enhance visual appeal and add green walls and tunnels to your garden or even your balcony

Container gardening is another option for maximizing yields in limited spaces. From simple terracotta pots to large stacked planters, container gardening offers you flexibility. You can choose the size of the containers according to the specific needs of your plants and available space. They can be placed strategically to optimize sunlight exposure and drainage. The beauty of container gardening is its adaptability.

Raised beds offer many advantages, especially in less-than-ideal soil conditions.
Building raised beds allows you to control the soil composition, ensuring the best possible conditions for your plants. Weeding and harvesting is also easier. For

Karen Blakeman

small spaces a narrow-raised bed against a wall or fences maximizes space. Let's not forget about companion planting. It is another useful strategy in toxic-free gardens improving the overall health and production.

Companion planting takes advantage of the synergistic relationships between different plants. Meaning they help each other grow and deter destructive insects. You see, certain plants repel pests or attract beneficial insects, activity of your garden. For instance, basil planted near tomatoes re- pels tomato hornworms, while marigolds deter nematodes. Onions keep pests away from berry bushes, and rosemary repels carrot flies and other pests. Research companion planting strategies to optimize your personalized garden's productivity.

Gustavo Fring

Crop rotation is critical for maintaining soil health and preventing the buildup of pests and diseases. If vine borers get into your pumpkins one year, replanting the same type of crop in that space will generally result in a repeat of the prior season. Rotate your crops annually, ensuring that different plant families occupy the space each year. This helps break disease cycles and prevents the depletion of specific soil nutrients. A well-planned rotation will keep your soil healthy and your crops thriving.

Then we have **succession planting**, which extends the harvest season by planting crops at different times. It keeps your garden full and thriving the entire planting season. As one crop finishes, another takes its place. This ensures that a continuous supply of fresh produce is available in the garden during all seasons.

Plan your succession planting carefully and keep an eye on the maturity times of your chosen crops. For a longer growth period, plants like Brussels sprouts and potatoes should be planted first, followed by crops like radishes that can be grown and harvested quickly.

Choosing the right seeds or seedlings is also crucial. Look for dis- ease-resistant varieties that are adapted to your specific climate and growing times. If you are living in the Pacific Northwest, you will have a shorter season than someone in the Southeast.

Start seeds indoors to get a head start on the growing season, in the south allowed me to start my bell pepper and tomato seeds indoors in mid-January.

Water your garden wisely. Drip irrigation and soaker hoses minimize water waste. To prevent disease, try to avoid overhead watering. Healthy gardens also need pest control. Here is where companion planning again comes into play. By planting certain herbs and flowers like Bee Balm, Marshmallow, and sunflowers you will attract beneficial pollinators to your garden. Certain insects, like ladybugs, will feast on aphids and mites. Try using other organic methods alongside companion planting, like insecticidal soap and neem oil.

Diatomaceous earth, a natural substance made from fossilized di- atoms, is a sharp powder that dehydrates and kills insects upon contact. Keep an eye on those weeds to help keep plants thriving.

Harvesting at the correct time is important for maximum flavor and quality of your produce. Harvest vegetables when they are fully ripe, but before they become overripe and begin to show signs of rot.

Write down your planting dates, harvests, and any challenges or successes you encounter. This will be a great reference for planning your next growing season. Learning from your mistakes and successes is all a part of successful gardening.

Remember, it's not about the size of your garden, but the efficiency of your methods. Even a small, well-planned garden can provide a huge amount of your family's fresh produce!

It will boost your confidence, help you in being more self-reliant and bring a sense of accomplishment. Not to mention putting delicious homegrown food on your table.

Selecting the Right Plants For Your Climate and Needs

Pixabay

Now comes the fun part, considering your personal needs and preferences! What do you and your family enjoy eating? Do you have a particular fondness for tomatoes? Are you a salad lover? If you don't like broccoli, don't grow it just because it's considered a staple. Focus on the plants that will actually be eaten.

This is where you personalize your self-sufficient garden. Don't feel obligated to grow only the most commonly grown vegetables. But before you start planning an orchard of Paw Paw trees in Colorado, let's talk about climate. Think about your specific region.

> **What's your average annual rainfall?**
> **What are your typical high and low temperatures throughout the growing season?**
> **Do you experience harsh winters, scorching summers, or something in between?**

These factors will significantly influence your plant selection and how it will flourish.

A tropical fruit tree won't thrive in a zone prone to frost, and a hardy winter squash will be very unhappy in a consistently humid climate. Knowing your USDA Plant Hardiness Zone is a fantastic starting point.

You can find this out online or at your local garden center. Your zone tells you the average minimum winter temperature in your area. Think of it as a guide for which plants can survive your win- ters or summers.

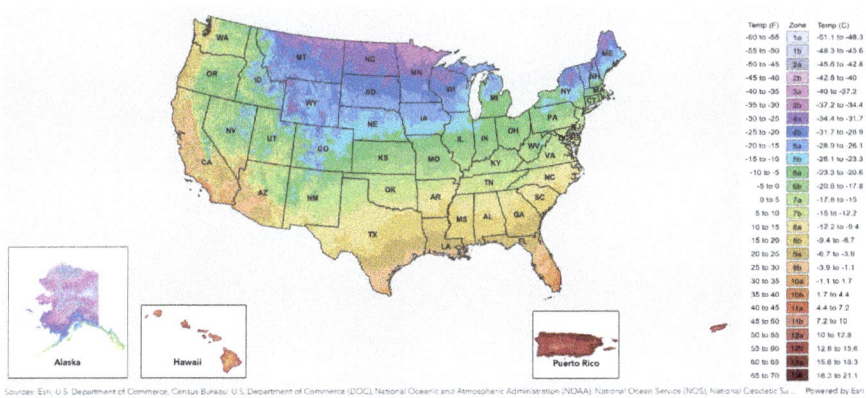

2023 USDA Plant Hardiness Zone Map

You will also want to consider herbs with multiple uses. Basil is a wonderfully versatile herb. It can be used for pesto, to flavor olive oil, and let's not forget its medicinal properties. It's fantastic for digestive and respiratory health. Rosemary is great for flavoring, is an anti-inflammatory and analgesic, and works as a natural pest deterrent.

This strategic planting approach allows you to maximize your gar- den's use and space. Planting fruit trees or berry bushes, even in limited spaces, is possible.

Dwarf variety fruit trees are perfect for smaller gardens and can grow quite effectively in barrel containers. A single dwarf apple tree can yield a substantial amount of fruit. Wave goodbye to that grocery store produce aisle.

Now, do you have to grow all your own fruit and vegetables to be considered self-sufficient. No. Community with this lifestyle is so important. Barter and trade with other homesteaders and consider buying from local farms and farmers' markets. Basically, support local agriculture and businesses.

Compost: Essential Soil Nutrition

Denise Nys

Now, let's discuss the importance of organic matter. This is the lifeblood of healthy soil. Organic matter is anything derived from living organisms, including compost, well-rotted manure, leaf mold, and other natural materials. Incorporating organic matter into your soil offers a ton of benefits. It improves the soil structure and makes it easier for roots to penetrate the soil and for water to drain.

It increases water retention, helping to reduce the frequency of watering. It provides a slow and natural release of nutrients, feeding your plants throughout the growing season. Compost also encourages beneficial microbial activity. This means it creates a thriving ecosystem in your soil that supports your plant's growth and health. Composting is the heart of organic soil amendment. It's the process of turning recycled organic waste into a nutrient-rich soil enhancer.

Whether you choose to have a large backyard compost bin or a small countertop composter, adding composting to your daily life will help keep waste out of the landfills and lower your carbon footprint. Food scraps, yard waste, coffee grounds, even shredded newspaper and cardboard can all be transformed into "black gold." It will enrich your soil, improve soil structure, aeration, and water retention. All while providing a balanced supply of nutrients for your plants at no extra cost to you.

The amount of organic matter you need to add to your soil depends on your soil's texture and current condition. Sandy soil, which drains quickly and lacks water retention, will benefit from a large amount of organic matter.

Clay soil, which can become compacted and drains poorly, also needs a good amount of organic matter to improve the soil structure and aeration. A good rule of thumb is to add at least 2-4 inches of compost or other organic matter to your garden beds before planting.

Beyond composting, consider other sources of organic matter. Well-rotted manure, cow, chicken, your choice, is a fantastic source of soil nutrients.

Keep in mind the compost will need to be well-aged before being used, or it will burn your plants.

Leaf mold from fallen leaves can be added to the garden as it de- composes naturally. They are another excellent source of help to improve soil structure and drainage.

You can help amend your soil with commercially available fertilizers, but I always prioritize organic options whenever possible. Organic fertilizers, like bone meal (for phosphorus), blood meal (for nitrogen), and greensand (for potassium), release nutrients gradually and mimic the natural processes for a healthy ecosystem. They also improve soil health in the long term.

Unlike many synthetic fertilizers, which have negative impacts on soil structure and beneficial soil organisms, while adding pesticides and chemicals onto your food and into your body.

Now that your soil is properly prepared, it's time to start planting.

But don't just plant directly into soil without a plan. Know beforehand which plants will go where. The best way to ensure your seeds and seedlings get off to a strong start is to create raised beds or use a no-till method.

This method allows for a more natural and healthier growing environment.

Pixabay

Mulching after planting further enhances Mulching after planting further enhances benefits helping the soil to retain moisture, suppress weeds, and regulate soil temperature.

Remember, preparing the soil is an ongoing process. Regular soil testing, composting, and the addition of organic matter will keep your garden thriving year after year. Think of your soil as a living organism that needs constant care, feeding, and attention. By treating it well, you'll be rewarded with abundant harvests.

Basic Gardening Techniques
Planting Watering and Pest Control

The trifecta of a successful garden is planting, watering, and pest control. Daily plant care ensures a healthy garden and a larger har- vest.

Your garden's success depends on understanding each plant's needs. First, carefully study the seed packet or plant tag. These will be your guide to proper spacing, planting depth, and soil condi- tions.

Ignoring these instructions risks overcrowding, stunted growth, or a dead garden.

Direct sowing is a straightforward method. It's perfect for beets, green beans, peas, beans, carrots and lettuce. Simply scatter the seeds according to the package instructions, cover them with a light layer of soil and water gently. Starting seeds indoors is a great option for plants that need a longer growing season, like peppers and tomatoes, or are more slow to start.

Daria Obymaha

Following these steps will lead to success: Using **seed starting mix**, rather than your garden soil, ensures the best possible drainage for fragile seedlings.
Remember to **keep the soil moist** but not waterlogged. We are not teaching our seedling to swim.
Provide **plenty of light**, whether through a sunny window or grow lights.
Once seedlings have developed a few **true leaves,** they can be successfully transplanted into your garden beds.

Transplanting established seedlings or nursery-bought plants re- quires a bit of finesse. Dig a hole slightly larger than the plant's root ball, gently remove the plant from its container, loosen the roots slightly, and place it in the hole. Fill the rest of the hole with soil, pressing firmly but gently around the base to eliminate air pockets.

Water thoroughly to help the roots settle. Sounds easy enough? Don't stress over it and don't allow others to over-complicate it. This is supposed to be relaxing and peaceful.

Water plants in the morning to allow foliage to dry throughout the day, preventing fungal diseases. Use a gentle watering method like a rose head watering can, a rain setting on your hose head, or drip irrigation.

Check the soil moisture before each watering. Wilting leaves usually indicate underwatering; while yellowing or browning leaves can be a sign of over-watering. Adjust your watering schedule accordingly, always prioritizing the needs of your plants. Mulching around your plants can reduce the frequency of watering and help keep weeds at bay.

Pest control is often viewed as a chemical battle, but self-sufficient gardeners try using more sustainable choices. Prevention is always the best approach. Healthy plants are more resistant to pests, so maintaining a well-balanced soil, proper watering, and good air circulation are essential. Choosing pest resistant varieties can also help reduce pest problems.

Check your plants regularly for signs of pests or diseases. Early detection can often prevent a minor problem from escalating into a major infestation. Handpicking pests from plants is a simple and effective method for small infestations. A strong spray of water with dish soap can dislodge many insects, too.

Finally, don't forget about crop rotation which we discussed previously. Rotating your crops each year helps to break the life cycles of many pests and diseases and prevents build up in the soil.

Rotating crops also helps maintain soil fertility by diversifying nutrient demands.

Remember, successful gardening is a continuous learning process. If something you have done failed, be willing to adapt. Don't be afraid to experiment, to try different methods, and to learn from your successes and failures. Embrace the challenges and the rewards.

And remember, a little humor goes a long way in the garden.

Harvesting and Storage Techniques for Fresh Produce

After watering and waiting for months it's time to harvest! But simply plucking a vegetable from the vine isn't the whole process.

Correct harvesting techniques are recommended for maximizing yield and ensuring the quality of your produce. It's important to understand the proper way to harvest each crop, since this significantly impacts flavor, texture, and the shelf life of your produce.

For many vegetables, the best time to harvest is determined by size and maturity. For example, lettuces are typically ready for harvest when the leaves are fully developed but before they begin to bolt. Meaning when flowers appear.

Harvesting before bolting ensures tender, flavorful leaves. Root vegetables like carrots, turnips, and beets are usually ready for harvest when they've reached the size indicated on the seed packet or plant tag. If you leave them in the ground longer than recommended, it could lead to woody textures, possible splitting, and a loss of flavor.

Some vegetables, like bush beans and zucchini, should be picked on a regular basis. Harvesting bush beans encourages continued production. Basically, the more you pick the more they grow.

Zucchini is notorious for its rapid growth and should be harvested frequently. Picking them from their vines while they are on the smaller side will keep them from becoming tough and seedy. The practice of regular harvesting, often referred to as "successive harvesting," is the foundation for maximizing your yield.

Basically, it keeps the plant's focus on producing more. The number one goal of the plant is to grow fruit and drop a seed to create another plant. By allowing fruits and vegetables to mature beyond their peak, you are allowing the plant to think it has accomplished its mission and stop producing.

Tomatoes, on the other hand, require a slightly different approach. Harvest tomatoes when they've developed their characteristic color and have a slight give when gently squeezed.

Green tomatoes can be harvested and ripened indoors but won't develop the same level of sweetness and flavor as those allowed to fully ripen on the vine. If there is a chance the tomato will split, pick it and ripen it on your windowsill. Also, if you pick your tomatoes in the morning, after the dew has dried, it prevents damage and disease from spreading.

Remember they don't do well in the refrigerator. Their flavor be- comes compromised by the low temperatures. They are best stored at room temperature in a single layer to allow for proper air circulation.

The ideal time to harvest herbs depends on the type of herb. Some herbs, like basil, are best harvested by pinching off leaves from the top of the plant. This encourages bushier growth and a continual supply of leaves.

Other herbs, such as rosemary and thyme, can be pruned more aggressively. Always use clean, sharp tools for snipping herbs to avoid damaging the plant.

When you harvest your crop be sure to use sharp knives or shears. For root vegetables, gently loosen the soil around the roots before carefully pulling them up to avoid breaking or damaging them.

And as for delicate greens, use scissors or a knife to cut the leaves at the base, rather than pulling them.

Properly clean and remove any soil or debris from your harvested produce. Wash delicate items gently. For heartier vegetables like carrots, a more thorough scrubbing may be necessary. Look for signs of damage, disease, or pest infestation. Discard damaged pro- duce.

Once you have your fresh produce cleaned and ready, the next hurdle is extending its shelf life. Proper storage techniques significantly reduce waste and ensure you can enjoy your harvest for as long as possible. The key is understanding the unique storage needs of different types of produce.

Some vegetables, like leafy greens, are stored best in airtight containers or plastic bags in the refrigerator's crisper drawer. This maintains moisture and prevents wilting. The crisper drawer's higher humidity helps to keep the leaves fresh for several days but keep an eye on them and remove any leaves that are starting to wilt, or it will spread and ruin the whole batch.

Other vegetables, such as carrots and potatoes, should be stored in a cool, dark, and dry place.

Never store potatoes and carrots together. This can negatively impact the quality of both vegetables. A root cellar is ideal, but if you don't have one, a cool spot in your basement or a well-ventilated crisper drawer in the refrigerator will do the job.

Soft fruits like berries and peaches are best eaten fresh as soon as possible, but you can extend their life slightly by storing them in the refrigerator in a single layer or preserving them. Avoid piling them on top of each other, or you may wind up with puree.

Harder fruits like apples and pears can be stored in the refrigerator for a longer time, but select ripe, firm fruits to store for the long term. Apples produce ethylene gas, which can hasten ripening in other fruits, so store them away from more sensitive produce.

Herbs will last longer in a glass of water on the kitchen counter or wrapped loosely in a damp paper towel or a plastic bag inside the refrigerator. Experiment with what works best for you.

Making a simple chart can be helpful in organizing your storage strategies. Keep a running inventory of what you have, where it is stored and when it was harvested. This will help prevent waste and ensure that you use your homegrown produce before it spoils.

Remember, these are just guidelines. The actual shelf life of your produce depends on multiple factors, including the ripeness at harvest, storage conditions, and the inherent variability of your pro- duce. Observe your stored produce regularly; a watchful eye is the best way to prevent spoilage.

Harvesting and storing your homegrown produce is a crucial part of the self-sufficient lifestyle. It's a skill that refines with practice, rewarding you with both delicious food and a deep satisfaction in your ability to provide for yourself.

Four

Herbal Remedies & Natural Body Care

Creating Your Own Medicinal Garden

Creating a thriving herbal medicine garden is deeply rewarding. It is a blend of horticultural skill and ancient wisdom. It's more than just growing pretty plants. You are creating a resource that can support your health and wellness in a natural, chemical-free, toxin- free, and sustainable way.

But before you even think about planting, let's talk about planning again. A well-planned medicinal garden can minimize wasted space, giving you the most natural medicine.

Start by considering the space you have available. Most of my medicinal flowers are planted in a garden at the front of my house. After choosing the most useful herbs and flowers for my family, I carefully laid out my design plans by looking at the height, color, and how far each plant would spread. Even though it was labeled stick figure flowers, I had a pretty good idea of what placement I was looking for.

Even a small balcony or a sunny windowsill can accommodate a surprisingly large amount of herbs. Especially if you utilize vertical gardening techniques like hanging baskets or tiered planters.

Most herbs thrive in at least six hours of direct sunlight daily, al- though some prefer partial shade. Well-drained soil is another key factor and can be easily accomplished with container planting.

Next, research which herbs best suit your climate, growing conditions, and family needs. Hardy herbs like rosemary, thyme, and lavender tolerate drought and can even withstand freezing temperatures in some cases. More delicate herbs such as basil and mint require warmer temperatures and consistently moist soil.

Consider the specific needs of each herb when planning the layout of your garden. You might even want to create different zones within your garden, grouping herbs with similar water and sunlight requirements together.

Begin with a small selection of versatile herbs, focusing on those that will serve multiple purposes. Chamomile, for example, is well known for its soothing properties, making it suitable for tea and compresses for skin irritations.

Lavender boasts calming aromatherapy qualities and can also be used in potpourri, added to bath products, or tea. Calendula is a stunningly bright orange flower that's also a powerful antiseptic and ideal for topical use.

Purple Cone Flowers, better known as Echinacea, is one of the most powerful herbs to fight colds and flu while strengthening your immune system. These are just a few examples. The possibilities are truly endless.

Remember to always source your herb seeds or plants from a reputable supplier. This ensures you obtain high-quality, correctly identified plants, minimizing the risk of accidentally planting something toxic or ineffective.

Ethical sourcing also supports sustainable agricultural practices and protects biodiversity. Avoid purchasing plants from untrusted sources.

Planting your herbs is fairly straightforward. Most herbs prefer well-drained soil, so be sure your planting area is prepared properly. If you use containers, choose pots with drainage holes to pre- vent water logging. Plant your herbs at the recommended spacing to allow enough room for them to grow and flourish. After planting, water thoroughly and consistently, but avoid over-watering, which can lead to root rot.

Regular maintenance is key to a thriving herbal garden. This includes weeding, mulching to retain moisture and suppress weeds, and providing support for taller herbs if needed. Regular harvesting encourages continued growth and prevents herbs from bolting or flowering prematurely.

Harvesting your herbs is an art in itself. The best time to harvest often depends on the herb in question. Generally, leafy herbs are best harvested in the morning, after the dew has dried but before the heat of the day has caused the essential oils to evaporate. Cut or pinch off stems and leaves, taking care not to damage the plant.

Proper drying and storage are crucial for preserving the medicinal properties of your herbs. Freeze-drying or dehydrating is an option if you have the equipment. If not, air drying is the traditional method, and I often choose. It ensures the herbs retain their essential oils. Tie a bunch of herbs together and hang upside down in a cool, dark, and well-ventilated area until completely dry.

Once dry, store the herbs in airtight containers to maintain their potency. Herbs can also be frozen and used in cooking. But remember that freezing can sometimes impact the delicate compounds that make herbal medicine effective.

Identifying herbs correctly is very important. Misidentification can have serious health consequences, so it's important to develop your plant identification skills and use only herbs you have identified positively. Reliable books, websites, and even local herbalists can be invaluable resources. When in doubt, be cautious and leave the herb alone.

Beyond the practical aspects of growing and harvesting, creating an herbal medicine garden has a spiritual element. Nurturing these plants, watching them grow, and benefiting from their healing properties creates a connection with nature and a deeper understanding of one's own body and its needs.

Let's look at some specific examples:

Chamomile (Matricaria chamomilla): Part of the Asteraceae family. It is known for its calming and anti-inflammatory properties. Chamomile is a must-have in any herbal medicine garden. Plant it in a sunny location with well-drained soil. Harvest the flowers when fully open, carefully removing them from the stems. Chamomile tea is a soothing remedy for indigestion and anxiety.

Lavender (Lavandula angustifolia): Believe it or not lavender is part of the mint family. The beautiful purple flowers of lavender are not just visually appealing; they also have potent antiseptic and anti-inflammatory properties. Lavender thrives in sunny, well-drained locations. Harvest the flowers during the peak of their bloom, ensuring they are fully open and fragrant. Lavender essential oil is often used for aromatherapy, while the dried flowers can be added to bath salts or potpourri.

Calendula (Calendula officinalis): This bright orange flower is also known as a pot marigold and has remarkable wound-healing properties. It thrives in sunny locations with well-drained soil. Harvest the flowers when fully open, ensuring the petals are bright and vibrant. Calendula cream or ointment can be made from these flowers and used to soothe minor burns, scrapes, and skin irritations. Calendula also makes a beautiful and fragrant addition to bath teas.

Mint (Mentha): A highly versatile herb, mint is a valuable addition to any garden, especially for those who appreciate it's refreshing flavor and aroma. It is best harvested int he morning and requires moist soil and partial shade. Harvest the leaves regularly to encourage new growth Mint tea is excellent for digestive issues, while the leaves can be used to flavor food and drinks. Several different mint varieties are available, each with its unique flavor and healing properties.

Flowers: Pixabay

Echinacea (Echinacea pupurea): A powerful immune booster. Echinacea, or cone flower, is in the daisy family and is known for its ability to help fight off colds and flu. It thrives in full sun and well-drained soil. Harvest the flowers when they are fully open. The roots and aerial parts of the plant are generally used to make tinctures and teas.

Remember, herbal remedies should be used with caution and ide- ally under the guidance of a qualified healthcare professional.

While many herbs are generally safe, certain herbs can interact with medications or have potential side effects, particularly if used in high doses. Never self-diagnose or self-treat serious medical conditions with herbal remedies.

Always consult with a qualified doctor or herbalist before using herbal remedies, especially if you are pregnant, breastfeeding, or taking any other medications.

Cultivating an herbal medicine garden is all about learning and discovery. Creating an herbal medicine garden has been a rewarding journey, both for my physical health and my spiritual well-being.

The front garden of my house now boasts a beautiful display of medicinal flowers, carefully chosen for their use and visual appeal. Nurturing my plants and witnessing their growth has helped me develop a deeper connection with nature. I understand their unique properties and how they support my health.

So, start small, plan wisely, and enjoy the fruits—or rather, the herbs—of your labor! As you gain experience, expand your collection. It is okay to experiment with different herbs and techniques. The world of herbal medicine is huge and offers endless opportunities for learning and growth.

Basic Herbal Preparations Infusions, Tinctures and Salves

Karolina Grabowska

Your herbal garden is planted and growing. It's time to learn how, while these preparations have been used for centuries, it's critical to approach herbal medicine with respect and caution.

Always consult a qualified healthcare professional before using herbal remedies, especially if you have pre-existing conditions or are taking other medications. Not to sound redundant, but I cannot stress this enough.

Let's start with **infusions**, the simplest of herbal preparations. Think of infusions as herbal teas. They're made by steeping herbs in hot water, but not boiling water, to extract their beneficial com- pounds. Boiling water can degrade some active ingredients, so aim for a temperature around 180°F-200°F (82-93°C). This process allows for relatively mild preparation, making infusions ideal for sensitive individuals or for internal use where a gentler approach is preferred.

To make an infusion, simply add a tablespoon or two of dried herbs or a handful of fresh herbs to a cup of hot water. Let it steep for 10-15 minutes, then strain the liquid through a fine-mesh sieve or cheesecloth. You can enjoy the infusion warm or allow it to cool completely.

Some herbs, like chamomile, can be enjoyed warm before bed for their relaxing properties. While peppermint can be refreshing served chilled. Experiment with different herbs and ratios to find your favorite combinations. Remember to label your infusions clearly with the name of the herb and the date of preparation to ensure freshness and accurate identification.

Next, let's explore **tinctures**, a more concentrated form of herbal medicine. Tinctures are made by extracting the active compounds of herbs using alcohol. The alcohol acts as a solvent by drawing out the plants' essential oils and other beneficial constituents. The process results in a potent and shelf-stable treatment that can be stored for long periods of time.

There are several ways of making tinctures, but the most common involves combining freshly harvested herbs or high-quality dried herbs with a high-proof alcohol, such as vodka or brandy. The ratio of herb to alcohol is typically 1:5, which is one part herb to five parts alcohol. However, this can vary depending on the herb and desired strength.

Here is how simple it is;

Place the herbs and alcohol in a clean, airtight glass jar. Make sure the herbs are completely submerged.

Seal the jar and store it in a cool, dark place for 3-4 weeks, shaking it daily to ensure proper extraction.

After the recommended steeping period, strain the liquid through cheesecloth or a fine-mesh sieve, squeezing out as much liquid as possible from the herb material.

Store the tincture in a clean, dark glass bottle with a tight-fitting lid. If stored properly, tinctures can last for several years.

When making tinctures, it's important to know your alcohol and what type of alcohol is required. Alcohol with at least 40% proof by volume is necessary for effective extraction and preservation.

Also, remember to always clearly label your tinctures, indicating the herb's name, the date of preparation, and the alcohol percent- age.

Finally, let's take a peek into the world of salves. Salves are topical herbal preparations that offer numerous skin care benefits. They are typically made by combining herbal infusions or tinctures with an oil base and beeswax. The oil provides a carrier for the herbal extracts, while the beeswax adds structure and helps the salve solidify.

To make a basic salve, start by making an infusion of your chosen herb. This infusion will serve as the herbal component of your salve.

Next, combine the infusion with a base oil such as olive oil, coconut oil, or shea butter. Then, add it to your beeswax. Melt the beeswax and oil together in a double boiler or a heat-safe bowl set over a pot of simmering water.

The ratio of oil to beeswax will determine the consistency of the salve. A higher proportion of beeswax will result in a firmer salve, while a lower proportion will create a softer, easier-to-spread product. Once melted and thoroughly combined, slowly add your cooled herbal infusion and stir gently until completely incorporated.

Pour the mixture into clean, sterilized tins or jars. Allow the salve to cool and solidify completely before sealing and labeling.

When making salves, be mindful of the potential for allergic reactions. Always test a small amount of the salve on a small area of skin before applying it liberally. Pay close attention to any reactions that may occur. The use of high-quality ingredients is very important. If you have not grown the herb yourself, I advise using organic and sustainably sourced materials.

Like tinctures, accurately labeling your salves with the ingredients and date of preparation is essential for safe and effective use.

Remember that herbal remedies are not a substitute for all medical treatments. While they can offer complementary support for various health conditions, it's crucial to consult a healthcare professional to diagnose and treat any major medical issues. Some herbs may interact with medications, so disclose your use of herbal remedies to your doctor.

Finally, practice good hygiene when preparing your herbal remedies. Use clean equipment and sanitize your work area to avoid contamination. Properly store your herbal preparations and always label your containers clearly with the name of the herbs, the date, and any relevant usage instructions.

You may think you will remember what is in each jar, but more than likely, as time goes by, you will forget. I know that I have.

By following these guidelines and taking the necessary safety precautions, you can turn your herbal garden into an all-natural medicine cabinet. By studying each herb and practice you can create effective and beneficial remedies for your well-being and add another skill to your self-sufficient lifestyle.

DIY Natural Body Care Products
Soap Shampoo and More

Pixabay

Have you ever considered making your own natural body care?

Today's commercial products are filled with junk. Forget the long lists of unpronounceable chemicals and toxins found in commercially produced soaps, shampoos, and lotions that will seep into your skin and make you sick. Instead, we can protect ourselves and our loved ones and create our own.

Using simple, readily available ingredients, you can reap the re- wards of healthier skin and hair while saving money on expensive products and minimizing our environmental impact. If you can follow a recipe, then it's surprisingly easy.

Let's start with **soapmaking**. It is an ancient craft of transforming oils and lye into a cleansing marvel. While it might sound intimidating, soapmaking is pretty straightforward. The key is understanding the basic chemistry and taking necessary safety precautions. Above all, follow the recipe directions!

Saponification is the chemical reaction between fats or oils like olive oil, coconut oil, or almond oil.

Olive oil soap is known for its moisturizing properties, while coconut oil creates a soap with excellent lather. Palm oil contributes to a hard bar of soap. Customize your oil to what you want in a soap. The oil is added to a strong alkali, typically lye (sodium hydroxide). Lye is caustic, so it's imperative you wear protective gear.

What kind of gear? Heavy vinyl or latex gloves, eye protection, and long sleeves should be worn throughout the soapmaking process. A well-ventilated area is necessary, but outdoors would be optimal. An open window is acceptable if you do not have an outdoor area. Never inhale lye dust or fumes.

Right here, most people would write off soap making. It's too dangerous, it's too intense, or it's too complicated. If you follow the correct safety protocol and recipe, it will go smoothly. I urge you to give it a try.

There are several methods for soapmaking, but the most common for beginners is the cold process method. This involves mixing measured amounts of oils and lye and creating a mixture that gradually saponifies over time.

The process begins with carefully measuring the oils and lye using a kitchen scale. Precise measurements are essential for successful soapmaking and unprecise measurements can result in a soap that's too harsh or too soft.

Once the oils and lye are measured, we gently combine them, stir- ring constantly until the mixture reaches a specific trace. This "trace" is a visual cue indicating the saponification process has begun. The mixture will thicken slightly, and when you drizzle a small amount from a spoon, it will leave a temporary trail on the surface.

This stage is critical. It determines the consistency of your soap. After reaching the trace, essential oils are added for fragrance and therapeutic benefits. Lavender, chamomile, tea tree, and rosemary are popular choices, each with its own unique properties.

Remember to use essential oils specifically designed for soapmaking. Some essential oils can react negatively to lye or lose their scent, so it's always best to make sure the essential oil is compatible with soap making. You can also add other ingredients like flowers, herbs, clays, or exfoliants like luffa, oatmeal, or coffee grinds.

Once the soap mixture is thoroughly combined, it is poured into a mold. Wooden molds are a classic choice, but silicone molds are equally effective and easier to clean. After pouring, the mixture must sit untouched and cure.

The process typically lasts four to six weeks, allowing the saponification process to complete and the soap to harden. During this curing period, the soap loses excess water and becomes firmer and milder.

Once cured, the soap is ready to be unmolded and cut into bars. Due to its water content, the newly made soap will be slightly softer than commercially produced soaps.

The final product is a luxurious, chemical-free soap that's gentle on your skin. Experiment with different oil blends and scents to create your own signature soap. Finding the perfect combination will result in your perfect soap match.

Moving on to **shampoo**! We can create our own natural alternatives to commercial products. Many commercial shampoos contain harsh sulfates and silicones that can strip the hair of its natural oils, leaving it dry and brittle.

Then there is formaldehyde, which is a known human carcinogen. Phthalates can also be in your haircare products and are known to change hormone levels and function, decrease sperm count, and increase the chance of gestational diabetes. Natural shampoos, on the other hand, can cleanse without the harsh effects of chemicals, leaving hair softer, healthier, and shinier.

One of the simplest natural shampoo recipes uses a blend of castile soap and essential oils diluted in water. Simply combine a small amount of castile soap with a few drops of your favorite essential oils and dilute it with water to the desired consistency.

This gentle shampoo is suitable for most hair types, especially those prone to dryness or damage. You can add a small amount of honey or aloe vera gel for added conditioning.

Another option involves using herbal infusions as a rinse. Using infusions of herbs like rosemary or chamomile as a final rinse after washing your hair with a mild cleanser can improve hair health and add shine and softness. The herbs themselves are rich in vitamins and minerals that nourish the scalp and hair.

You can use natural ingredients to moisturize and protect your skin for lotions and creams. Shea butter is a natural powerhouse. It offers intense hydration and nourishing properties. Coconut oil and tallow are my personal choice for my dry skin, and they are excel- lent for moisturizing the skin and are quickly absorbed.

Combine these oils with essential oils for fragrance and therapeutic benefits. Add some honey to keep the skin hydrated. Honey is an antibacterial and has anti-inflammatory benefits. By making your own lotion, you can create a truly personalized moisturizer.

To make a simple **lotion**, gently melt shea butter, coconut oil, or both in a double boiler or heat-safe bowl over simmering water. Once melted, add a few drops of your preferred essential oils. Stir until well combined, then allow the mixture to cool and solidify. This simple balm is surprisingly effective. It will leave your skin feeling soft, smooth, and nourished.

Remember that creating your own body care products can be more like an experiment. Some recipes may not suit you. And that is okay! Don't be afraid to try different combinations of oils and herbs to find the perfect blend for your specific needs.

Enjoy the process. When you find the perfect combination for your needs, savor the satisfaction of knowing exactly what ingredients went into the products you use on your hair and skin.

The beauty of self-sufficiency is not only in the tangible results but also in learning, experimenting, and connecting more deeply with nature and your own resourcefulness.

Seriously, how awesome is it that you made your own natural HBA products? You'll not only be saving money but also con- tributing to a healthier environment and a healthier you! The rewards are well worth the effort.

Essential Oils Uses and Safety Precautions

Essential oils are the fragrant distillates of plants and flowers. They offer a wealth of benefits. The oils are taken from aromatic plants' leaves, stems, roots, bark, or flowers through steam distillation or other extraction methods.

These potent oils capture the plant's scent and medicinal proper- ties, offering a concentrated dose of its therapeutic properties in the oil.

However, it's important to understand proper use and safety pre- cautions. Improper use can lead to negative reactions, so finding and correctly applying a reputable source are important.

One of the most popular uses of essential oils is in aromatherapy. Basically, you inhale essential oil vapors. It is said that essential oils can affect the limbic system and the part of the brain responsible for emotions and memories, for stress reduction, mood elevation, and promoting relaxation.

Diffusing essential oils is a simple and effective method. A few drops of oil added to a diffuser disperse the oil into fine particles, transforming a room's atmosphere. Lavender is widely used for its calming and sleep-promoting properties.

Chamomile can help ease anxiety, and peppermint can provide a refreshing and invigorating boost and help alleviate headaches. Al- ways ensure you use a diffuser specifically designed for essential oils.

Another effective aromatherapy technique involves the inhalation method. A few drops of essential oil can be added to a bowl of hot water. This will create a steam inhalation. Covering your head with a towel will allow you to inhale the vapors deeply. This method is particularly useful for clearing congestion and easing respiratory issues.

Eucalyptus, peppermint, and tea tree essential oils are frequently used due to their decongestant and antiseptic properties. However, always be careful that the water is not too hot to avoid burns. Al- ways test a small amount on your skin to check for any potential allergic reactions.

Essential oils have many topical applications in skincare. Many essential oils possess antibacterial, antifungal, or antiviral properties, making them valuable additions to skincare routines. Remember that essential oils are highly concentrated and should always be di- luted in a carrier oil before applying them to your skin.

Carrier oils, such as soap bases, coconut oil, olive oil, or sweet almond oil, and tallow serve as a base to dilute the essential oils and prevent skin irritation. A general guideline is to use a ratio of 1%-3% essential oil to carrier oil. For example, you would add 3-9 drops of essential oil for a one-ounce bottle of carrier oil.

Tea tree oil is a popular choice for its antibacterial and antifungal properties, making it effective for treating minor skin blemishes and infections.

Myrrh oil is known for treating skin issues and athlete's foot.

Rose Hip is high in antioxidants and vitamin C. It possesses anti-inflammatory properties and is known to help reduce scars.

Lavender oil is known for its soothing and calming effects on the skin, making it suitable for treating minor burns, cuts, insect bites and promotes sleep.

Rosemary oil can help stimulate hair growth, making it beneficial for scalp treatments. It also helps reduce tension and fatigue.

Hyssop oil can be used to help decrease inflammation and minimize scarring.

Again, always perform a patch test before applying any essential oil blend to a large area of skin, especially if you have sensitive skin or a history of allergies. Observe the area for any signs of irritation or allergic reactions for at least 24 hours before applying it to a larger area.

There are so many oils and combinations of oils to choose from with diverse healing properties. Adding a few drops of essential oil to your favorite lotions, creams, or soaps can enhance their fragrance and add therapeutic benefits.

Rosemary
Teona Swift

Myrrh
Pexels

Aloe Vera

Rose Hip
Eva Bronzini

Hyssop
Pixabay

Remember to always thoroughly mix the essential oils into the base product to ensure even distribution. Adding essential oils to homemade bath bombs, salt scrubs, or shower gels can create an aromatic self-care experience.

Let's address the responsible sourcing of essential oils. Look for high-quality essential oils from reputable suppliers who practice sustainable harvesting and ethical production methods. Look for oils that are certified organic or wildcrafted whenever possible. Quality does affect the quality of the product. Read the labels carefully, they will provide valuable insight into the oil's origin and ex- traction methods. Honestly, as the saying goes, "you get what you pay for" is very true with essential oils. Don't forget that a little bit of oil goes a long way.

Finally, let's discuss essential oil safety precautions. The most critical aspect is dilution. I know I have said this before, but never ap- ply undiluted essential oils directly to the skin. Doing this can cause skin irritation, allergic reactions, or even burns. Always dilute them in a carrier oil before topical application

Additionally, some essential oils are phototoxic, meaning they can increase the skin's sensitivity to sunlight. Avoid applying these oils before sun exposure. Examples include citrus oils like lemon, lime, bergamot, and grapefruit.

Avoid using essential oils internally unless explicitly instructed by a qualified healthcare professional. Certain essential oils can be toxic if ingested. Pregnant and breastfeeding women should exercise extreme caution and consult a doctor or qualified aromatherapist before using essential oils.

Children, elderly individuals, and those with existing medical conditions should consult their physician before using any essential oil. Always keep essential oils out of reach of children and pets.

Essential oils should be stored in dark, airtight containers in a cool, dark place away from direct sunlight and heat. Proper storage will help maintain the oils' quality and potency. If you experience any adverse reactions, discontinue use immediately

And consult a doctor.

In summary, while essential oils offer a wide array of benefits, re- sponsible usage, including dilution and patch testing, is wise for ensuring both safety and effectiveness. Embrace the fragrant world of essential oils but always prioritize safety and informed application.

Essential oils can be successfully integrated into a self-reliant lifestyle when used correctly. From creating your own soothing aromatherapy blends to improve your health, to crafting natural skincare and body care products. The rewards of using essential oils safely and effectively are significant, offering a pathway to a healthier life.

Understanding Natural Ingredients and Their Properties

Understanding the intricacies of natural ingredients is akin to unraveling a mysterious puzzle. It is this knowledge that forms the foundation of creating powerful yet safe remedies and body care products. It is not enough to merely follow instructions and recipes blindly. You see, true mastery lies in understanding the "why" behind each product and the unique properties of each ingredient.

Every ingredient has a story to tell. By studying their characteristics, we can unlock their potential and create something truly remarkable. It is a delicate balance of science, nature, and chemistry, it is this synergy that is truly amazing.

Are you driven by the desire to not only create effective remedies but also to use the sustainable gifts the natural world provides? The world of herbal remedies and natural body care is making a come back into our overly commercialized and immediate gratification lifestyle.

Each new creation is an adventure. It is a chance to discover the unknown and share the wonders of nature's medicine with those seeking a holistic approach to their well-being.

Let's start with some common herbs and oils found in many home remedies.

Calendula is a star performer in skincare. Its vibrant orange petals are packed with compounds that promote wound healing, soothe irritated skin, and reduce inflammation. You will find calendula in salves, creams, and even infused oils. It's gentle enough for even sensitive skin, but always do a patch test first, just to be on the safe side.

Chamomile is a classic remedy for soothing anxieties and promoting restful sleep. But its benefits extend beyond calming the mind. Chamomile tea, made from its delicate white and yellow flowers, is a gentle digestive aid and is often used to help with in- digestion and upset stomachs. Topically, it can soothe irritated skin and reduce inflammation, making it a useful addition to skincare products. However, some individuals might be allergic to chamomile, so caution is advised, especially for those with rag- weed allergies.

Aloe vera is an easy-to-care-for succulent plant with thick, fleshy leaves. It is a powerhouse of natural healing. The gel extracted from its leaves is known for its soothing and healing properties. It's a natural moisturizer, effective in treating sunburn, dry skin, minor wounds, and even acne. It contains various compounds with anti- inflammatory and antibacterial properties, making it a valuable ad- dition to skincare products and herbal remedies. Avoid using aloe vera on deep wounds or severe burns. It is best for superficial skin issues.

Moving on to the world of oils, we find a treasure trove of benefi- cial properties.

Coconut oil is a staple in my household. But it is more than just used for cooking. It's a fantastic moisturizer for both skin and hair.

It offers deep conditioning and protection. Its antibacterial and an- tifungal properties make it useful in treating minor skin infections. However, be aware that it can be comedogenic for some, meaning it might clog pores, so those with oily or acne-prone skin should use it with caution.

Jojoba oil, on the other hand, closely mimics the skin's natural se- bum. This makes it an excellent moisturizer that won't clog pores.

It's non-comedogenic and great for all skin types, even sensitive ones. It's also a fantastic carrier oil for essential oils, helping to dilute them for topical use. It balances oil production, making it a great choice for treating acne and other skin conditions.

Olive oil is one of my favorite oils. It is a culinary staple and known to aid in weight loss, but also holds skincare secrets. Its rich fatty acids nourish and hydrate the skin, making it an effective moisturizer. It's particularly beneficial for dry or mature skin. The anti-inflammatory properties can soothe irritated skin and are great in homemade hair masks for conditioning and shine.

Now, let's explore some common ingredients used in natural body care products.

Shea butter is extracted from the nut of the African shea tree. It is a rich and creamy moisturizer that deeply nourishes and softens the skin. It's packed with vitamins and fatty acids that protect the skin from environmental damage. It is a perfect treatment for dry skin, eczema, and even stretch marks.

Cocoa butter is another rich, luxurious butter and is similar to shea butter in its moisturizing and nourishing properties. It is known to improve skin elasticity, making it a popular choice for treating stretch marks and scars. Its rich texture also makes it a fan- tastic addition to lotions and lip balms.

Beeswax is a natural wax secreted by honeybees and is a versatile ingredient in natural cosmetics. Yes, this is the same beeswax that is used to make candles. It adds structure and stability to lotions, creams, and lip balms and gives them a firmer consistency. It also has protective and emollient properties that help to retain moisture and protect the skin from environmental stressors.

Let's not forget about the humble **clay**. Yes clay. Different types of clay, such as bentonite and kaolin clay offer unique properties. Bentonite clay is known for its absorbent and detoxifying properties and is used for face masks. It can help to draw out impurities and excess oil from the skin. Kaolin clay, on the other hand, is gentler and more suitable for sensitive skin. It has soothing and calming properties and is frequently used in gentle facial cleansers and masks.

These natural ingredients merely scratch the surface of the world of herbal remedies and natural body products. The more you learn, the more empowered you'll become to create products that suit your individual needs and preferences.

Five

Sustainable Practices for the Home

Reducing Waste Composting and Recycling Strategy

Ben Kerkx

Reducing waste is all a part of sustainable living. Composting is at the top of the list. It's not only about reducing your environmental impact but also about converting kitchen scraps and yard waste into a valuable nutrient rich compost that will feed your gar- den. Whether you have a large backyard or a small balcony, there's a composting method that will fit your space.

Let's begin with the basics of composting. Let me start by saying do not compost meat and dairy! It attracts orders, pests and can create potential bacterial contamination.

Composting is the natural process of decomposing organic matter. This involves breaking down materials like food scraps, vegetable peels, coffee grounds, eggshells and yard waste like leaves, grass clippings, shredded paper and cardboard. The magic happens through the work of microorganisms like bacteria, fungi, and other beneficial critters that thrive in a moist and oxygen rich environment. These microorganisms break down the organic matter and transform it into a dark and crumbly substance filled with nutrients.

For those fortunate enough to have a yard, a traditional compost pile or bin is a fantastic option. You can construct a simple com- post bin from available materials like pallets or chicken wire. I purchased a pre-made bin from a garden center that rotates. It's the perfect size for my small backyard.

The key to good compost is to maintain proper airflow and moisture levels. A good rule of thumb is to layer "greens" that would be nitrogen rich materials like grass clippings and food scraps and "browns" the carbon-rich materials like dried leaves and twigs to ensure a balanced decomposition process. Try for a roughly equal ratio of greens and browns.

Regular turning of the pile helps to aerate it and speeds up the de- composition process, preventing unpleasant odors. Keep the pile moist, like a damp sponge, but not soggy. Overly wet piles become anaerobic, that means lack oxygen and leads to a sticky compost pile and slow decomposition.

Now, what about those of us living in apartments or without access to a backyard? Fear not! Composting is still entirely possible. Do you like worms? Well from here on out worms are your new best friends! Worm composting, or vermicomposting, is an incredibly efficient way to compost in small spaces.

All you need is a worm bin which is readily available online or at garden supply stores. These bins typically consist of layers to hold your worms and provide drainage. Red wiggler worms are ideal for vermicomposting. They are voracious eaters and thrive in a dark and moist environment.

Just add food scraps to the bin and your worms will do the rest. The resulting worm castings, or worm poop, are an exceptionally rich fertilizer. They are the golden ticket for gardeners due to their high nutrient content and soil improving properties.

Another excellent apartment friendly composting method is Bokashi composting. Bokashi uses effective microorganisms (EM), beneficial bacteria and yeasts to ferment food scraps. This method allows you to even compost items that would typically at- tract pests in traditional composting, like meats and dairy.

It creates a nutrient rich, fermented material, that can be buried in the garden or added to a regular compost pile. Bokashi composting produces a slightly acidic byproduct like chicken poop that is useful but needs further composting to fully break down.

Composting food scraps, even on a small scale reduces landfill waste and provides valuable and free fertilizer for your garden.

A vitamin, mineral rich and chemical free compost that will feed and enrich your garden will lead to healthier and more vibrant plants. This, in turn, enhances the fruits and vegetables you are growing and creates tastier and healthier food.

It's basically a cyclical process. You create a mineral filled com- post, feed your garden, it keeps waste out of the landfills and in turn, feeds you. You see, the journey toward self-sufficiency is about using your resources and creating a more meaningful connection with nature.

Reducing landfill waste is a important part of sustainable living and proper recycling is a crucial part of that. Research your local recycling guidelines. They are different from region to region, so knowing what materials your community accepts is essential.

Commonly recycled materials include paper, plastic, glass, and aluminum. Be sure to rinse and clean containers before recycling to prevent contamination.

Keep in mind that recycling alone isn't a total solution. By reducing our consumption of single use plastics and other non-recyclable items we can make a huge difference in reducing plastic pollution.

Try using reusable bags, re-usable water bottles, and glass food containers whenever possible. Make conscious choices to buy products with minimal packaging. Whenever feasible, purchase loose produce. Bring your own reusable bags or containers to the grocery store or farmer's market to reduce the need for plastic bags.

This practice not only minimizes plastic waste but also helps reduce your overall packaging waste. Supporting local farmers' markets is not only good for the environment but also a fantastic way to connect with the community and source fresher produce.

While many communities now have recycling programs for plastic bags, the process is often inefficient and many bags end up in land- fills anyway. The solution? Reusable shopping bags. Keep a set of sturdy, washable bags in your car, by your door, and even in your purse. Choose durable bags made from natural fibers like cotton or canvas. They're not only ecofriendly but also far more stylish than their flimsy plastic counterparts. Support local businesses commit- ted to sustainability and reducing their environmental impact.

Even small changes can have a significant effect. One day I decided to stop buying paper napkins. I slowly integrated cloth nap- kins and eliminated paper napkins from mealtimes. Now my family doesn't even look for a paper napkin. Embracing a more sustainable lifestyle often feels like a monumental task, but it's easily achievable with small, incremental changes.

Choosing reusable food containers over single use plastic bags can also make a big difference. Glass containers are an excellent choice and my go to. They are durable, easy to clean, and don't leach chemicals into your food.

Silicone food wraps are another great option. They are flexible, reusable, and washable. Beeswax food wraps are an ideal sustainable and natural alternative plastic wrap.

Sandwiches, fruit and bread are just a few items that can be wrapped in them. They are pliable so you can also cover bowls. Properly storing food is crucial to reduce spoilage and reduce your need to buy new supplies so often.

Plastic water bottles are a classic example of landfill waste. Invest in a high-quality reusable water bottle made from stainless steel or BPA-free plastic. Not only will you be reducing plastic waste, but you'll also likely find that you drink more water throughout the day. Filling up your reusable bottle is also an excellent way to reduce plastic consumption when you are out and about. How about ditching those plastic disposable straws for reusable metal ones?

Smalls steps will lead to larger changes in your lifestyle.

Don't be discouraged if you don't get everything right from the start. This is your journey into self-reliant living. You should celebrate your successes along the way. Learn from any and all mistakes. It's a process of refining your habits and finding what works best for you and your family.

The transition to a more sustainable lifestyle requires mindful choices and a change in mindset. It's about making conscious decisions to reduce our consumption, minimize waste, and prioritize the use of reusable items.

This also means understanding the lifecycle of products and making informed decisions about purchase. Ask yourself: Do I really need this? Can I borrow or rent it instead of buying? Is there a more sustainable alternative available? By asking these questions, we can significantly reduce our carbon footprint.

Incorporating composting and recycling strategies into your daily routine is an important step towards living a more self-reliant life. These practices minimize your negative environmental impact and provide a sense of accomplishment knowing that you're actively contributing to a healthier planet.

Pexels

Minimizing Plastic and Paper Use

Gerd Altman

Moving on to paper. While it's often considered a more biodegrad- able alternative to plastic, excessive paper consumption still pre- sents an environmental challenge due to the energy and resources required for its production. Think trees. We can drastically cut down on paper waste with simple lifestyle adjustments.

For instance, go for digital bill pay and bank statements rather than paper copies. Many companies now offer this service. Borrow books from the library or consider purchasing e-books and digital magazines instead of print copies. Even though the e-readers and tablets themselves have environmental impacts, the reduced use of paper in the long run makes a significant difference.

Household items are undergoing a transformation, abandoning their paper-based formats for a more traditional choice. Change from paper towels to cloth towels. Not only are they more environmentally friendly, but they're also more absorbent and durable.

Keeping a stack of designated cleaning rags made from old clothing or towels will allow for reuse many times before being com- posted or repurposed.

How about ditching paper napkins for cloth napkins? This switch might seem small, but over time, the impact is substantial.

Packaging is another major source of waste. Before you purchase anything, take a moment to examine the packaging. Choose products with minimal packaging or packaging that is easily recyclable. Support companies that prioritize sustainable packaging options.

Look for products sold in bulk or in reusable containers to minimize waste. Buy products in glass or cardboard over plastic pack- aging if you have the option. This small change can result in a significant reduction of waste over time. Read the product labels carefully and become more aware of the materials used in the packaging.

Beyond reusable alternatives and mindful shopping, there are several other strategies to help minimize plastic and paper consumption. Think about your own personal paper usage.

Questioning your personal needs can help you make informed decisions that minimize consumption, helping to reduce both plastic and paper waste. This philosophy can help you reduce your impact on the environment.

Composting food scraps and yard waste further reduces the need for additional paper or plastic bags. If you are composting your food scraps, you won't need to use additional plastic garbage bags to store the materials. Likewise, if you are using yard waste for compost, you won't need additional paper or plastic bags to dispose of your yard clippings.

Composting can help eliminate the need for additional paper and plastic materials altogether. This approach is not only a self-sustainable mindset, but it will also save you money in the long run.

Remember, the transition to a more sustainable lifestyle is a gradual process. Starting where you are with one or two changes, will gradually incorporate more changes as you become more comfortable. Don't strive for perfection. None of us are perfect.

Strive for ongoing progress. This effort will ultimately help to secure a healthy planet for future generations. The journey towards sustainable living is a rewarding endeavor that benefits us all.

Energy Conservation and Water Efficiency

Embracing sustainability extends beyond minimizing waste. Let's think about consciously managing our consumption of natural re- sources like energy and water. This can be a geographical worry. A friend of mine who moved to the southeast from California was amazed at how we used water here. From her own experiences with droughts she thought we were wasting water. She and her children would wet their hands when washing them, turn the water off soap up and scrub. Then, turn the water back on and rinse their hands.

While my husband and I just left the water running while we washed. Observing this made me stop and wonder. Was I wasting precious resources and how can I be more conscience of my natural resource use?

Karolina Grabowska

Water and energy are fundamental to our daily lives and their efficient use impacts both our wallets and the environment. Let's explore some practical strategies for conserving both energy and water in our homes.

Energy conservation begins with keeping an eye on our appliances. Energy-efficient appliances that are marked with Energy Star ratings are a wise investment. While the initial cost might seem higher, the long-term savings on electricity bills are substantial.

The higher the rating, the more energy efficient the appliance is. This is particularly crucial for appliances we use regularly, like refrigerators, self-standing freezers, washing machines, and dryers. Consider replacing older and less efficient models with a modern Energy Star equipment. This upgrade can lead to a reduction in your energy consumption and your electricity bill.

Remember when Mom would yell, "Turn the lights out! I'm not supporting the power company!" It's still true today. Lighting drains our overall energy consumption significantly. Switching to LED bulbs is a simple and impactful change. LEDs consume less energy than incandescent and CFL bulbs while producing comparable lighting. LEDs are also longer-lasting.

While the initial cost of LED bulbs may be slightly higher, they pay for themselves with reduced energy usage and extended lifespan. In addition, installing dimmer switches can further reduce energy usage by controlling the intensity of your lighting. By allowing you to adjust the brightness according to your needs, you could use less energy.

The use of natural light is another effective way to reduce reliance on artificial lighting. Open those curtains and blinds during the day!

Allow the sunlight to shine into your home. Consider using light colored reflective paints and materials in your interiors to maximize the reflection of natural light. This simple technique can significantly brighten your home and minimize the need for electric lighting.

Here is another energy sucker. Heating and cooling. This accounts for a large amount of household energy that is used. For us in the south, our central air systems are as important to us as heat is to those in the middle of a winter storm in Montana.

That's why proper insulation is crucial for maintaining a comfort- able indoor temperature while minimizing energy loss. Check the insulation levels in your walls, attic, and basement.

Be sure that there are no gaps or cracks that allow for heat or cool air to escape. Improve insulation where necessary to prevent heat loss during winter and cool air loss during summer.

Investing in good insulation is a long-term investment that saves energy and money.

Heating and cooling systems themselves also play a critical role in energy efficiency. Regular maintenance of your heating and cooling system is imperative. This includes changing air filters regularly, scheduling annual maintenance, and addressing any issues promptly. A well-maintained system operates more efficiently and requires less energy.

Consider programmable or smart thermostats to automate temperature control. These thermostats can learn your habits and adjust the temperature accordingly, saving energy while maintaining comfort. This technology allows for greater control over temperature and re- duces energy wastage while you are not at home.

Try unplugging electronic devices and appliances when not in use, or cut power to multiple devices with a power strip. This simple act prevents what's known as "phantom load," which is the energy consumed by devices in standby mode. This small change can lead to considerable savings over time.

Moreover, adopt energy-conscious habits in your daily routine. For example, take shorter showers, pull out that clothesline and air dry clothes whenever possible, and avoid using energy-intensive appliances during peak time periods.

Water conservation is equally important. There is an increasing scarcity of fresh water in many parts of the world. Practicing water saving techniques in your home is essential for environmental reasons but also for reducing water bills. Switching to a low-flow showerhead and faucet are an excellent starting point. These fixtures reduce water flow without compromising water pressure.

Low-flow toilets use less water per flush compared to standard toilets, allowing significant water reduction over time.

Second to the bathroom, kitchen water use needs to be observed. Avoid letting the water run continuously while washing dishes.

Wash dishes in full sinks instead of running water continuously. Wash your vegetables in a bowl rather than under running water.

Suppose you are able to install a low-flow dishwasher. Modern dishwashers use sophisticated water-saving technology, which leads to saving a large amount of water waste.

Outside, maybe you could install a rain barrel to collect rainwater for use in watering your garden or plants. This not only conserves water but also utilizes a valuable natural resource. Efficient irrigation methods can reduce water waste in outdoor areas. Avoid over- watering your lawn by using smart irrigation systems or watering only when necessary.

Water plants early in the morning or late in the evening to minimize evaporation. Using drip irrigation or soaker hoses for targeted watering rather than sprinklers, which tend to waste water through evaporation and overspray, is a great option. These careful irrigation practices will reduce your water usage and help your plants thrive.

Regularly check for leaks in your plumbing system. A small, seemingly insignificant leak can waste a huge amount of water over time. Address any leaks quickly to minimize water loss.

Repairing these minor issues can significantly reduce your overall water usage and save you money on your water bill. Regular checks for leaks are a proactive step that can help avoid bigger problems down the line.

These efforts, combined with conscious consumption, contribute significantly to a sustainable and self-reliant lifestyle.

DIY Cleaning Products and Household Maintenance

Let's shift our focus to another area of sustainable living. Cleaning. We are talking about doing so without resorting to harsh chemicals that pollute our soil and potentially harm our health.

Making your own cleaning products is simple, rewarding, and, dare I say, even fun! Forget brightly colored plastic bottles promising miracle spot removal. You can achieve sparkling results with ingredients you likely already have in your pantry without poisoning yourself or your family.

The beauty of DIY cleaning lies in its simplicity and customization. You're in control of the ingredients. You are ensuring they're safe for your family, pets, and the planet. Many commercial cleaners contain harsh chemicals that can irritate skin, contain cancer- causing ingredients, trigger allergies, and contribute to indoor air pollution.

By creating your own solutions, you eliminate these concerns and breathe easier knowing you're using gentle, effective, and environ- mentally friendly products. Plus, you'll save money in the long run. It is a win-win for your health and your wallet.

Pexels

Let's start with a **multi-purpose cleaner** that's a real workhorse. This recipe is so versatile that it can tackle most cleaning jobs around the house. You will need white vinegar, water, and essential oils for scent. Combine equal parts white vinegar and water in a spray bottle.

The vinegar's acidity cuts through grease and grime remarkably well, while being completely biodegradable.

If you're sensitive to vinegar's scent, just add a few drops of your favorite essential oil, like peppermint, lavender, lemon, or tea tree These oils not only add a pleasant fragrance but also offer additional cleaning and antimicrobial properties.

This simple mixture is great for cleaning countertops, sinks, floors, and even windows. Be sure to test on a small inconspicuous area first to ensure it doesn't damage the finish.

For tougher messes, you might want to increase the concentration of vinegar. For particularly stubborn stains or grease buildup, try a solution of two parts vinegar to one part water and a tablespoon of baking soda. This stronger mix will provide extra cleaning power without resorting to harsh chemicals. Remember to always test any cleaning solution on a small, hidden area before applying.

Particularly on delicate surfaces like wood or polished stone. A little preventative testing goes a long way to avoid accidental damage.

Next, let's tackle **bathroom cleaning**. One of the most common problems is soap scum buildup in showers and tubs. For this, baking soda is a valuable ally. Baking soda is a mild abrasive, meaning it can scrub away grime without scratching surfaces. Make a paste by combining baking soda with a small amount of water to form a thick consistency.

Apply this paste to the affected areas and let it sit for a few minutes to allow the baking soda to work its magic, then scrub with a sponge or brush. Rinse thoroughly with water. For particularly stubborn soap scum, add a bit of white vinegar to the baking soda paste. The fizzing action will help to loosen and remove even the most stubborn buildup.

For **cleaning toilets**, a simple solution of baking soda and vinegar can work wonders. Pour a generous amount of baking soda into the toilet bowl, followed by a cup of vinegar. The fizzing reaction will help loosen and remove stains and grime. Let it sit for about 30 minutes, then scrub with a toilet brush. For persistent stains, you can repeat the process or even leave the solution overnight for more effective cleaning.

Now for cleaning the **floors.** The type of floor will dictate the best cleaning method. For hardwood floors, a mixture of warm water and a few drops of dish soap is usually sufficient. Avoid using excessive water as it can damage the wood. For tile floors, the multi- purpose vinegar solution mentioned earlier works well.

For **carpets**, consider using a homemade carpet cleaner. Mix baking soda with a small amount of water to form a paste, and sprinkle it over the carpet. Leave it to sit for several hours or even overnight to absorb odors and stains. Then vacuum thoroughly.

Regular cleaning is essential inside and outside. But preventative maintenance is even more effective. For example, regular inspection of your gutters and downspouts prevents water damage to your house foundation and landscaping.

Cleaning out gutters twice a year, in spring and fall, is a simple yet crucial maintenance task. Clogged gutters can lead to water over- flow, causing damage to the roof, walls, and foundation of your house. It will also interfere with your water harvesting efforts. This preventative maintenance saves you from potentially expensive re- pairs down the line.

Maintaining your appliances is equally important. Regular cleaning of your refrigerator coils improves its efficiency and reduces energy use. Cleaning the lint trap in your dryer after each use pre- vents fire hazards and ensures efficient operation.

Regular maintenance of your heating and cooling system, as mentioned earlier, including filter changes and annual inspections, is essential for both safety and energy efficiency.

These small but regular maintenance tasks ensure the longevity and efficient operation of your appliances, saving you money and energy in the long run.

Another often-overlooked aspect of household maintenance is window care. Clean windows not only enhance the appearance of your home but also allow for maximum natural light penetration.

Cleaning windows regularly, at least twice a year, will help to maintain their clarity and allow sunlight to illuminate your home more effectively. This simple act contributes to both energy saving and improved home aesthetics.

While we advocate for environmentally friendly practices, it's important to address pest infestations effectively. Natural pest control methods, such as diatomaceous earth, neem oil, or essential oils, can be highly effective against common household pests. These natural remedies are safe for your family and pets while being environmentally friendly. They are also often significantly cheaper than commercially available pest control products.

It's important, though, to use these methods correctly and to identify the pest accurately before starting treatment. Sometimes, even natural pest control might not be sufficient, and you might need to contact a professional pest control service. The key is to find a balance between effective pest control and environmentally responsible practices.

By combining regular cleaning, preventative maintenance, and natural pest control methods, you create a healthy and sustainable home environment for yourself and your family. Remember, sustainable living isn't about drastic measures. It is a journey towards making small, conscious choices that add up to a big difference.

Sustainable Home Repairs and Upcycling Project

Now that we've covered cleaning and basic maintenance, let's jump into the creative world of sustainable home repairs and upcycling projects.

We are not just about patching things up or adding a "band-aid." It is about embracing a mindset of extending the lifespan of your belongings. It's about seeing the potential in that old dresser; others see a piece of trash.

Think of it this way, every item you repair or repurpose an item, it is a small victory against the relentless tide of consumerism.

You're reducing waste, saving money, and even developing valuable skills. Plus, there's a certain charm in reusing a piece of furniture, a tool, or even a piece of clothing that carries history and a story. It is a testament to your resourcefulness and commitment to sustainability.

Let's start with some typical household repairs. One frequent culprit for discarded items is broken furniture. A wobbly chair leg? A loose drawer? These are often easily fixable. A quick trip to your hardware store for wood glue, screws, and possibly some wood filler can work wonders!

But before you head out, take a minute or two to look at the dam- age. A few well-placed screws may be all you need fix that chair. Wood glue, used correctly, can create powerful bonds. For more significant damage, wood filler can seamlessly patch holes and cracks.

YouTube is a treasure chest of instructional videos. If you search for "wood repair techniques," you'll be surprised at the variety of solutions available. You can often repair relatively extensive dam- age with a little patience and the right materials.

Remember, before you even consider a repair, always check for loose screws or any easily fixed problems first. Often, a simple tightening is all it takes to restore functionality. Once the problem is found you can decide on the proper repair solution.

Moving on from furniture, let's address clothing repairs. A rip or a missing button might seem like a reason to throw an item away, but most of the time, these are minor issues easily remedied with a needle and thread. Mending clothes is a wonderfully calming and practical skill to learn. It's a skill that our immediate gratification type culture has forgotten.

Thanks to countless online tutorials, ranging from simple repairs to more advanced techniques like patching and darning, this art has not fallen into extinction. These skills aren't just useful. They can be very relaxing. Think of this as a way to become more thoughtful of your self-sufficient lifestyle. Allow yourself to slow down and appreciate the process of giving new life to old items.

Now, let's take a look at the world of upcycling. This is where your real creativity will come in. Old jars become quirky storage containers, perfect for holding spices, buttons, or even homemade candles. Old T-shirts can be cut and sewn into cleaning rags, reusable shopping bags, or even whimsical quilts. The possibilities are truly endless.

Here's my favorite upcycle. Think old pallets. These are often dis- carded, but with a little sanding and creativity, they can be trans- formed into beautiful shelves, headboards, or even outdoor furniture. A neighbor made a bar in their garage out of pallets.

If you plan to make something to go inside just be sure to check that the wood is appropriately treated before bringing it indoors.

You will want to avoid any pest issues. Online forums and Pinterest are brimming with inspiring ideas and step-by-step instructions.

Another fantastic upcycling project involves old jeans. Faded or ripped jeans can be turned into shorts, a handbag, or even a potholder. Again, the internet is a goldmine of tutorials and inspiration. This is an excellent opportunity to be creative and put a little of yourself into each project. And what about those glass bottles you're constantly recycling?

Don't just toss them! They can make amazing candle holders or decorative containers. You could even paint them with fun designs. Perhaps using one as a vase to hold flowers from your garden.

Upcycling extends beyond just textiles and wood. Old metal containers can be repurposed as planters or storage solutions for tools. Broken ceramic pots can be mended using specialized epoxy de- signed for pottery or used as a unique decorative mosaic in your garden.

The key is to look at discarded items with a fresh perspective. To see beyond their current state and imagine their potential for a new life.

Beyond individual projects, consider the bigger picture. Sustainable home repairs and upcycling contribute to a much broader effort to reduce our environmental footprint.

Every time we choose to repair an item instead of replacing it, we're conserving resources, reducing waste, and lessening the demand for new products. This act, multiplied across households, represents a powerful collective action.

Think about the energy saved by not manufacturing a new product. What about the resources saved? The raw materials, the water, and the energy that are used daily in manufacturing and transportation? It's a ripple effect that goes beyond our homes.

The entire manufacturing and consumption chain is influenced. This broader perspective should reinforce our commitment to sustainable practices.

It's a tangible demonstration of our individual impact on a larger scale.

The process of repairing and upcycling is also a great way to build skills and be more resourceful. It's a great feeling knowing that you can take something broken or trashed and transform it into something valuable and beautiful. This sense of accomplishment goes beyond the practical. It encourages a sense of self-reliance and a deep connection to your belongings.

So, the next time you're faced with a broken item or you have a pile of things set aside for the trash, take a moment before taking it to the dump. Consider the potential for repair or upcycling. You may be surprised at what you can accomplish with a little creativity, ingenuity, and some basic tools. The rewards extend beyond the tangible results. You'll be saving money and learning new skills that will only help you in the future.

And honestly, isn't that a rewarding way to spend your day? Re- member that sustainable living isn't doing everything perfectly. Every small step, every repair, and every recycling project contributes to a more sustainable lifestyle. So go ahead, unleash your inner MacGyver. Your wallet, your home, and the planet will thank you.

For those who are scratching their heads in confusion, he was a character who could make a bomb out of chewing gum. And you will be amazed at the satisfaction you will have transforming discarded items into something useful.

You might even discover a hidden talent for crafting or home improvement along the way. So, get out there and get your hands dirty! Enjoy each step you take towards living a more sustainable and self-reliant lifestyle. This is an adventure that is worth taking.

One small repair and one upcycling project at a time. And who knows, you might even start a trend among your friends and neighbors like I did!

Six

Building Community, Sharing Skills

Connecting With Other Like-minded Individuals

Henning Westerkamp

Hopefully, I have cleared up the fact that living a more self-sustaining life is not about hiding out in the woods and avoiding other people. It is very much about building a strong support network. It is as crucial to a self-reliant lifestyle as growing your own vegetables or mastering basic home repairs.

In fact, connecting with like-minded individuals can seriously amplify your efforts and enrich your journey towards a more fulfilling and sustainable life. Think of it as a cooperative garden, where each member contributes their unique skills and experiences, resulting in a bountiful harvest for everyone.

The beauty of a community built around self-reliance is the sharing of knowledge and resources. Perhaps you're a whiz at sourdough bread making, while your neighbor is a master gardener with an overflowing vegetable garden. By connecting with each other you can trade sourdough loaves for fresh veggies. Begin to create an exchange that goes beyond mere bartering. It is fostering the spirit of community and mutual support.

Find your tribe! It can be easy, even if you live in a busy city. The internet offers a ton of opportunities to connect with others who share your same passion for sustainable living.

There are online forums, social media groups, and dedicated web- sites that provide platforms for exchanging ideas, seeking advice, and celebrating successes. These online communities often foster a sense of camaraderie and shared purpose. Sometimes it's just the encouragement you need to keep going for both beginners and seasoned homesteaders.

One of the best rewards of these online communities is the amount of available information right at your fingertips. Need advice on dealing with a specific pest affecting your tomato plants? Chances are, someone in the group has already faced the same challenge and has a toxic-free solution to share.

Do you struggle with your sourdough starter? Someone in the community may have a few recommendations to get that starter bubbly again. This shared knowledge is a huge advantage, saving you time, money, and potentially a lot of frustration.

Remember those old-fashioned skills we have been discussing? Many online communities are dedicated to preserving and reviving traditional crafts, from repairing furniture and clothing to preserving food.

You can find tutorials, tips, and tricks, and a welcoming community of people who are eager to share their knowledge with you. In time, as you learn more skills you will not just consume all the in- formation given but actively participate in an exchange of ideas. You will contribute your own knowledge and skills. So, listen and learn now.

The benefits of community can extend beyond the digital realm. Look into community gardens, local farmers' markets, and workshops. They all offer opportunities for face-to-face interaction. In fact, I recently attended a local farmers' market and had a 20-minute discussion about the vendor's plants and plans to sell other herbs.

These gatherings provide opportunities to exchange ideas, learn practical skills, and create real-life connections. Meeting people who share your values and passions can be incredibly inspiring and motivating. For myself, the online community has contributed so much to my personal knowledge of homesteading.

These communities give you a sense of belonging and support. More importantly, interactions can lead to unexpected opportunities for collaboration and resource sharing. Imagine bartering your excess homegrown produce for a neighbor's carpentry skills. This is a tangible demonstration of the collaborative spirit that defines a self-reliant community.

Have you ever considered joining a local community garden? These shared garden plots are perfect for learning from experienced gardeners, swapping seeds and plants, and sharing advice on pest control and other gardening challenges. The group effort involved in maintaining a community garden often develops into a strong sense of community and shared purpose.

It's a perfect setting for building relationships and exchanging skills beyond the realm of gardening. You might even learn a few new recipes using the garden's harvest!

Don't discount the power of local workshops. Many communities offer classes on a wide variety of self-reliance skills, from basic canning and preserving to more advanced techniques like cheese making or woodworking.

These workshops provide a valuable opportunity to learn from experienced instructors and meet like-minded people who share your enthusiasm for sustainable living. The hands-on experience is invaluable, solidifying the skills you learn and building your confidence.

Look for local meetups or groups related to sustainable living, homesteading, or permaculture. These groups often organize workshops, potlucks, and skill-sharing events. They may provide opportunities for you to connect with others and learn new skills in a relaxed and informal setting.

These informal gatherings can be a deep well of useful information and a great way to build genuine friendships based on shared interests. The shared experience of learning and growing together strengthens the bonds within the community, creating a supportive network that extends beyond any single skill or project.

Beyond specific groups, consider simply talking to your neighbors. You'd be surprised how many people are interested in sustainable living or have a hidden talent for a particular craft. A simple conversation can open unexpected opportunities for collaboration and mutual support.

Perhaps your neighbor is a skilled seamstress who can mend your clothes, or maybe they have a surplus of eggs or fresh produce they'd be happy to share. These spontaneous connections can lead to the most enriching relationships.

Building a community of self-reliant individuals isn't about finding a perfect group. It's about actively participating with the world around you and building connections. It's about recognizing the power of shared knowledge, mutual support, and collaborative efforts.

A sharing spirit is essential for both individual and collective growth and fosters a sense of belonging. Remember that sharing your knowledge is just as important as receiving it.

By contributing your expertise to the community, you're not just helping others; you're also reinforcing your own understanding and strengthening your skills.

The journey towards self-reliance is not a solitary activity. So, reach out and connect with others. Discover the remarkable strength and resilience that comes from building a supportive network of like-minded individuals. Shared enthusiasm can be infectious.

I love to help my friends and family be more motivated and in- spired. It's a great feeling when you have that sense of belonging. It makes the challenges of a self-reliant life much easier to get through. It's the power of teamwork and the rewards of sharing a journey towards a more fulfilling and sustainable life.

And let's be honest, sharing your homegrown tomatoes and sour- dough bread with friends is pretty great, too! The process of connecting and building these relationships is as rewarding as the skills themselves, adding a social and emotional dimension to your journey towards a self-reliant life. Enjoy the journey – and the company!

Sharing Your Knowledge and Skills with Other

Gustavo Fring

Sharing your hard-earned knowledge and skills not only benefits others but also reinforces your own understanding and deepens your appreciation for the craft. Think of it as a circle. The more you teach, the more you learn. It's a beautiful cycle of growth. And let's face it, there's a certain satisfaction that comes with proving others knowledge to achieve self-sufficiency. There is such joy in seeing a person's face light up after they have mastered a new skill.

One of the most effective ways to share your expertise is through teaching. This doesn't necessarily mean standing in front of a class- room and droning on and on. It can be as simple as showing a friend how to can tomatoes or showing them how to make a tincture.

You might be surprised at the level of interest and the enthusiasm your friends display once they see how simple some of these skills can be. Keep it fun. I taught two of my very good friends how to pressure can. We picked two recipes, and each got a portion of the ingredients, then made a reservation at a cabin with a beautiful view. We made a weekend of it! During that time, we shared the prep work, talked, laughed, and generally had a great time. We still talk about it to this day.

Additionally, don't be afraid to share your mistakes along the way. Your sourdough started to flop, it's okay. It makes the learning process more relatable and engaging. Your pie came out of the oven a gloppy mess. It's okay, start over. Your green beans didn't give you a big yield? Adjust the soil and replant them. You now have experiences and maybe a few solutions to share with others.

For those with a passion for sharing on a larger scale, consider teaching formal classes or workshops at local community centers, libraries, or even online. Many community organizations are looking for instructors to teach practical skills, and your expertise could be exactly what they're looking for!

You could develop a curriculum and create handouts and exercises to be used during the presentation. This will add to the experience for those attending. But remember, the key is to make it enjoyable. Incorporate anecdotes from your own experiences, inject some hu- mor, and encourage questions and interaction from the participants. Imagine yourself sitting in the workshop. We all know a lively, engaging class is far more effective than a dry lecture.

Remember, the goal isn't just to transfer skills. It's to keep the his- tory of self-sufficiency alive. It's to create a passion for self-reliance in others. To help give others confidence that they can live this lifestyle and not rely so heavily on government or consumerism. Sharing your passion allows for a deeper level of connection with others and often leads to lasting friendships based on shared interests and mutual respect.

No matter how you choose to share your new passion for home- steading with others, do it with honesty and patience. And yes, it is homesteading. Acres of land are not required to homestead.

It's a mindset and a way of living. Remember the feeling of accomplishment when you've mastered a new skill? The goal is to help others experience that same joy, empowerment, and independence.

Sharing your new skills can take many unexpected forms. Imagine offering a free sewing session at a local farmers' market. Perhaps you could organize a community canning day. Invite the neighbors to bring their own produce and learn the art of preserving food together while sharing the bounty.

Such projects provide a sense of community and build lasting relationships. Sharing the work to create something together will deepen the bonds within the community and give the community a sense of accomplishment. It could be a small project, like canning a batch of homemade pickles, or a larger project, like a community-crafted quilt.

Don't underestimate the value of simple gestures. Offering to help a neighbor with a small repair, sharing extra seeds from your gar- den, or providing a instruction on how to do a simple task can make a huge difference in someone's life.

This act of kindness can go long way in building your community while deepening your commitment to a self-reliant lifestyle by helping others achieve a greater level of independence.

In addition, consider documenting your skills and knowledge. Creating a resource guide or a series of instructional videos can pro- vide lasting value to your family and provide a legacy to future generations. You can play a part in preserving invaluable skills and a tradition that will continue to benefit future generations.

Be a Participant

Karen Blakeman

You could also participate in local initiatives and sustainable projects that extend the circle of self-reliance beyond your individual household. Recognizing true self-sufficiency isn't just about what you can do on your own property, but also about the strength and resilience of the community around you. By actively taking part in local projects, you not only contribute to a more sustainable future but also learn from others' expertise.

One highly rewarding avenue is to initiate a community garden if one is not available in your neighborhood. These spaces provide opportunities to share resources, exchange gardening tips, and collectively produce a bounty of fresh food. Imagine the camaraderie of working side-by-side with your neighbors. Then there is sharing the joy of harvesting ripe cucumbers or nurturing delicate seedlings.

Community gardens often develop a sense of shared ownership and responsibility, leading to a stronger sense of community. They also offer valuable learning opportunities. You will learn new techniques from other gardeners and share your own knowledge and questions. The benefit of fresh produce is enticing considering today's prices.

However, community gardens often incorporate elements of sustainable practices. Composting systems are frequently used, turning kitchen scraps and yard waste into valuable fertilizer. Water conservation strategies like rainwater harvesting and drip irrigation are often added to the garden.

The very act of growing food locally reduces the environmental impact associated with long-distance transportation. The cumulative effect of each of these actions contributes to a more environmentally conscious community.

Try participating in local farmers' markets. This vibrant activity connects producers directly with consumers, creating a sense of community and supporting local agriculture. Beyond simply buying your produce at a farmer's market, you could volunteer to help set up or take down the market.

You do not have to have a bounty of products or crafts to sell to participate. Offering your time and helping this operation run smoothly is just as vital as the vendors.

Another valuable initiative is to join or support local food banks and food recovery programs. These organizations work to reduce food waste and ensure that those in need have access to nutritious meals. You could volunteer your time to sort and distribute food, donate your excess harvest, or even help serve meals.

The act of sharing not only your extra produce but also your time is a powerful statement of community solidarity and a powerful display of the unbreakable bond of self-reliance. It's a reminder that self-reliance isn't about hoarding food and other resources but about sharing them wisely and compassionately with others.

Don't underestimate the power of community involvement. Gather those "tool hoarding" friends and organize a neighborhood tool library. Residents can borrow tools instead of buying them and reduce waste. This will help to promote resource sharing.

How about starting a seed swap? These small gatherings can have a significant impact on the community's sustainability and resilience. Your friends, family and neighbors can exchange seeds from their gardens. Not only will it promote biodiversity and you will also build friendships. Even organizing a community potluck fosters a sense of connection and celebrates the bounty of local food.

Have you thought of using local businesses that prioritize sustainable practices? This is also an important step towards building a more self-reliant community. By patronizing businesses that use eco-friendly materials, source their products locally, and prioritize fair labor practices, you are actively supporting a more sustainable economic model.

If you do this, you will help strengthen the local economy while reducing the environmental impact associated with long-distance transportation and mass production. It's a powerful way to demonstrate sustainability through your everyday choices.

Support Local Businesses and Sustainable Practice

Pixabay

Shopping at local businesses that believe sustainable practices is more than just a trend. One of the most impactful ways to support local, sustainable businesses is to simply shop locally. This might mean choosing to wait for the farmer's market over rushing right over to the supermarket. Using the local bakery over the national chain or visiting the town's bookstore over using the big box giant.

By consciously choosing to invest in local businesses you make a choice that aligns with your values. Each purchase you make is a silent affirmation of the values you hold dear. When you choose to spend your money locally, you're not just getting what you need; you are also investing in the community's economic future and adding support to a more resilient local food system.

But it's not just about where you buy. It's what you buy. Pay attention to the labels. Look for businesses that are transparent about their sourcing practices. Companies that use eco-friendly materials and prioritize fair wages for their employees. These businesses will often go the extra mile to minimize their environmental impact, using sustainable packaging, reducing waste, and supporting renewable energy sources Take, for instance, the local brewery that sources its hops from a nearby farm that uses rainwater harvesting to irrigate its crops and minimize its carbon footprint through efficient brewing processes.

Are you shopping at the clothing boutique that exclusively carries apparel made from organic cotton that was produced using ethical labor practices. Or are you buying from the woodworking shop that uses reclaimed lumber to craft unique furniture pieces with minimal environmental impact? These are the businesses that de- serve our support, businesses that embody the principles of sustainability and community building.

Don't underestimate the power of word-of-mouth marketing. Share your positive experiences with everyone! Tell your family and friends about products and services that stood out.

Spreading the word about the value they bring to the community and the quality goes a long way. Your recommendations can be far more influential than any advertisement. It's a simple yet powerful way to amplify the impact of your support.

By supporting local businesses, you're contributing to a more di- verse local economy. You are helping to create jobs, contributing to the local tax base, and reducing your reliance on large corporations and global supply chains. You're also gaining access to higher-quality, toxin-free products.

And finally, you're contributing to a community that reflects your ideals. Let's extend the principles of your home garden to the broader economic landscape. Just as you nurture your plants with care and attention, you can nurture your local economy by supporting businesses that share your same commitment to sustainability.

Finally, think about the impact of your personal spending habits. Each dollar that you spend is a vote for the type of world you want to live in.

I know that sounds a bit cheesy. But the long-term benefits of supporting local businesses creates a cycle that develops
a stronger and more resilient community for everyone.

You are not just helping them to survive, you're helping
them flourish, ensuring the continued prosperity of your
community for generations to come.

How great would it be if there were a whole community
where self-reliance isn't just an individual pursuit but a shared
endeavor?

Acknowledgments

First and foremost, a hearty thank you to my patient and supportive family, who endured countless nights of me muttering about bubbling jars of watered-down flour and the proper way to prune a fig tree (apparently, there's a lot to it.)

To my friends who are always on-board and ready to try out my crazy ideas.

A big shout-out to the online homesteading community – you guys are a well of knowledge, encouragement, and support.

To my readers - May your gardens flourish, your kitchens hum with activity, and your spirits remain bright. Here's to the messy, rewarding, and unbelievably fulfilling life of a self-reliant soul! Happy Homesteading!

Thank you for being so supportive. I would not be writing if it were not for readers like you! I hope this book has given you insight and confidence to move forward with your self-sufficiency dreams.

If you found "6 Ways To Live A More Self-Reliant Life" helpful, I would appreciate it if you could take a moment to leave a positive review where you purchased my book.

References

While this book draws heavily from my own experiences and accumulated wisdom and a few questionable internet forums, I have consulted the additional resources below and highly recommend them for those eager to dive deeper into the world of self-sufficient and self-reliant living.

Seymour, John *The Self-Sufficient Life and How to Live It* New York, DK Publishing, 2018

Deppe, Carol *The Resilient Gardener* New York, Chelsea Green Publishing Co., 2010

Bining, Melissa (2025 May 15) Easy Homemade Strawberry Jam with Pectin. "My Homemade Roots." https://myhomemade- roots.com/easy-homemade-strawberry-jam-with-pectin/

Rekstis, Emily (2018, July 3) Essential Oils 101: Finding the Right One for You. "Healthline." ttps://www.healthline.com/health/essential-oils-find-the-right-one-for-you#Types-of-essential-oils

Wallace, Zoey (2015, January 13) 24 Time-Saving Cooking Tips That Will Simplify Everything. "Chef Standards" https://chefstan- dards.com/time-saving-cooking-tips/ Zoey Wallace January 13, 1015

Eberhardt, Davin (2024, December 15) Homesteading without Land: 19 Ways to Start Today. "The Nature of Home." https://thenatureofhome.com/homesteading-without-land-19-ways- to-start-today

Author Biography

Renee McCorry is a passionate suburban homesteader, writer, and all-around enthusiast for living a more self-sufficient life. With years of experience in gardening, cooking, and crafting, Renee shares her knowledge and practical advice through her friends (even if it's unwanted) and books.

When not wrestling with unruly squash plants or trying to make that dress pattern work, she can be found strolling through Scottish Highland Games with her husband, spending time with her friends, children and grandchild and generally embracing the joys and challenges of a less than ordinary life. Renee lives in the southeast with her husband and fur baby.

Your feedback helps others discover this book and supports indie authors like me in continuing to share information and content on a lifestyle that could fade into extinction without sharing knowledge.